高等职业教育"十三五"规划新形态教材

实用英语拓展教程 1

主　编　刘　克　倪振伶
副主编　冯　岩　何冬芝　刘仲阳

北京理工大学出版社
BEIJING INSTITUTE OF TECHNOLOGY PRESS

版权专有 侵权必究

图书在版编目（CIP）数据

实用英语拓展教程.1 / 刘克，倪振伶主编. —北京：北京理工大学出版社，2018.6（2019.8重印）

ISBN 978-7-5682-5804-3

Ⅰ. ①实… Ⅱ. ①刘… ②倪… Ⅲ. ①英语–高等职业教育–教材 Ⅳ. ①H319.39

中国版本图书馆 CIP 数据核字（2018）第 139479 号

出版发行 /	北京理工大学出版社有限责任公司
社　　址 /	北京市海淀区中关村南大街 5 号
邮　　编 /	100081
电　　话 /	（010）68914775（总编室）
	（010）82562903（教材售后服务热线）
	（010）68948351（其他图书服务热线）
网　　址 /	http://www.bitpress.com.cn
经　　销 /	全国各地新华书店
印　　刷 /	三河市文通印刷包装有限公司
开　　本 /	710 毫米×1000 毫米　1/16
印　　张 /	12.25
字　　数 /	240 千字
版　　次 /	2018 年 6 月第 1 版　2019 年 8 月第 2 次印刷
定　　价 /	37.00 元

责任编辑 / 武丽娟
文案编辑 / 武丽娟
责任校对 / 周瑞红
责任印制 / 施胜娟

图书出现印装质量问题，请拨打售后服务热线，本社负责调换

编写说明

当前，高职英语教学应兼顾专业性与实用性相结合的原则，学生在教师引导下完成课堂教学任务的基础上，还应加强自我学习和自我检测。为此，我们结合学生的实际情况，编写了此教程。

该教程是主干教材强有力的补充，为学生课后第二课堂学习提供了明确的引导，方便学生对自己的英语水平进行自测和评估。同时，该教程还为课堂小测试提供便利，方便教师加强对学生的平时考核。

本教程共分十个单元和两套真题自测。每个单元包括词汇和语法、实用阅读、翻译、实用写作和两篇补充阅读文章。其中，实用阅读和翻译内容还可以用作口语训练内容，让学生强化英语口语。补充阅读文章可以让学生在巩固英语知识的同时，加强道德文化教育，强调"以德树人"的教育理念。

本教程由刘克、倪振伶担任主编，冯岩、何冬芝、刘仲阳担任副主编。该教程词汇和语法部分由冯岩老师编写，实用阅读一至五单元由刘仲阳老师编写，六至十单元由何冬芝老师编写，翻译和实用写作部分由倪振伶老师编写，补充阅读文章和两套真题自测由刘克老师编写。刘克和倪振伶老师负责全书的统筹和组稿。

由于时间紧迫，编写仓促，该教程在编写中难免有失误之处，敬请各位同仁批评指正，谢谢！

Contents

Unit One 1
    Part Ⅰ   Vocabulary & Structure 1
    Part Ⅱ   Reading Comprehension 2
    Part Ⅲ   Translation (English into Chinese) 7
    Part Ⅳ   Practical Writing 8
    Supplementary Reading 9

Unit Two 15
    Part Ⅰ   Vocabulary & Structure 15
    Part Ⅱ   Reading Comprehension 16
    Part Ⅲ   Translation (English into Chinese) 21
    Part Ⅳ   Practical Writing 22
    Supplementary Reading 22

Unit Three 29
    Part Ⅰ   Vocabulary & Structure 29
    Part Ⅱ   Reading Comprehension 30
    Part Ⅲ   Translation (English into Chinese) 34
    Part Ⅳ   Practical Writing 35
    Supplementary Reading 36

Unit Four 43
    Part Ⅰ   Vocabulary & Structure 43
    Part Ⅱ   Reading Comprehension 44
    Part Ⅲ   Translation (English into Chinese) 49
    Part Ⅳ   Practical Writing 50
    Supplementary Reading 51

Unit Five 58
    Part Ⅰ   Vocabulary & Structure 58
    Part Ⅱ   Reading Comprehension 59
    Part Ⅲ   Translation (English into Chinese) 64
    Part Ⅳ   Practical Writing 65
    Supplementary Reading 66

Unit Six ... 76
- Part Ⅰ　Vocabulary & Structure ... 76
- Part Ⅱ　Reading Comprehension ... 77
- Part Ⅲ　Translation (English into Chinese) ... 82
- Part Ⅳ　Practical Writing ... 83
- Supplementary Reading ... 83

Unit Seven ... 89
- Part Ⅰ　Vocabulary & Structure ... 89
- Part Ⅱ　Reading Comprehension ... 90
- Part Ⅲ　Translation (English into Chinese) ... 94
- Part Ⅳ　Practical Writing ... 95
- Supplementary Reading ... 96

Unit Eight ... 105
- Part Ⅰ　Vocabulary & Structure ... 105
- Part Ⅱ　Reading Comprehension ... 106
- Part Ⅲ　Translation (English into Chinese) ... 111
- Part Ⅳ　Practical Writing ... 112
- Supplementary Reading ... 112

Unit Nine ... 121
- Part Ⅰ　Vocabulary & Structure ... 121
- Part Ⅱ　Reading Comprehension ... 122
- Part Ⅲ　Translation (English into Chinese) ... 127
- Part Ⅳ　Practical Writing ... 128
- Supplementary Reading ... 128

Unit Ten ... 134
- Part Ⅰ　Vocabulary & Structure ... 134
- Part Ⅱ　Reading Comprehension ... 135
- Part Ⅲ　Translation (English into Chinese) ... 140
- Part Ⅳ　Practical Writing ... 141
- Supplementary Reading ... 141

高等学校英语应用能力考试（B 级）2016 年 12 月真题 ... 151

高等学校英语应用能力考试（B 级）2015 年 12 月真题 ... 162

Answer Key ... 173

参考文献 ... 186

Unit One

Part I Vocabulary & Structure

Section A

Directions: *In this section, there are 10 incomplete sentences. You are required to complete each one by deciding on the most appropriate word or words from the 4 choices marked A, B, C and D. Then you should mark the corresponding letter on the Answer Sheet with a single line through the center.*

1. Don't take the wrong turn before you _____ the railway station.
   A. have   B. run   C. keep   D. reach

2. The team doesn't mind _____ at weekends as long as they can finish the task.
   A. worked   B. working   C. to work   D. work

3. We are a non-profit company _____ team members are from all over the country.
   A. whose   B. that   C. which   D. what

4. The meeting room is so small that it can hold 20 people _____.
   A. at last   B. at first   C. at most   D. at once

5. She gave us a detailed _____ of the local government's new health-care proposal.
   A. impression   B. explanation
   C. education   D. communication

6. Linda _____ her training in a joint company by the end of next month.
   A. finishes   B. has finished
   C. had finished   D. will have finished

7. It was not until yesterday _____ they decided to re-open the business talk.
   A. when   B. which   C. that   D. as

8. We have to _____ the cost setting up a new hospital in that area.
   A. work out   B. put on   C. fill up   D. carry on

9. We need to _____ an eye on all the activities to make sure that people stay safe.

A. catch   B. keep   C. take   D. bring

10. The local government has always placed a strong emphasis _____ education and vocational training.

A. with   B. for   C. on   D. to

Section B

Directions: *There are 5 incomplete statements here. You should fill in each blank with the proper form of the word given in brackets. Write the word or words in the corresponding space on the Answer Sheet.*

11. We were impressed by the (suggest) _____ you made at yesterday's meeting.

12. The (long) _____ Charles has lived in this city, the more he likes it.

13. If you want to learn some terms related to your field, you will find this book might be (help) _____.

14. No one is allowed (smoke) _____ in public buildings according to new regulation.

15. The new president (ask) _____ some tough questions by the reporter in the interview yesterday.

Part II Reading Comprehension

Directions: *This part is to test your reading abilities. There are 5 tasks for you to fulfill. You should read the materials carefully and do the tasks as you are instructed.*

Task 1

Directions: *Read the following passage and make the correct choice.*

Last week as my husband and I were driving near the beach, we noticed a small house with a "For Rent" sign. We went onto the front porch and knocked at the door, but no one answered, so we walked down the steps and around to the rear of the house. There we found a small yard surrounded by a fence with an old metal gate.

Because the house was empty, we decided to take a look inside. We looked in one of the windows near the back porch and saw that the inside was dusty but generally in good condition. The walls and floors were in perfect condition. The only thing that needed repair was the ceiling in the kitchen, which had been damaged by some rain water.

While we were looking, a neighbour came over to see who we were. The house belonged to him, so he was able to take us inside. There was a total of six rooms, and all but the kitchen had carpeting. The house was unfurnished, but there were still several pictures hanging in one of the rooms. In general, the house looked wonderful.

The landlord explained to us that the rent was $350 per month, due by the fifth day of each month, and that usually he required a deposit equal to one month's rent. However, if we would repair the ceiling, he would not charge us the deposit. The idea sounded very good, so my husband and I went home to abandon things. We decided to take it.

1. The couple _____.
   A. drove to the beach for holidays
   B. happened to find a house for rent
   C. noticed a small house surrounded by a fence
   D. walked around, trying to find the back door of the house
2. There was a small yard _____.
   A. behind the house   B. in front of the house
   C. far from the house   D. near the house
3. Why did they think it was all right to take a look inside the house?
   A. Because the house was in perfect condition.
   B. Because the house was under repair.
   C. Because the house was untidy.
   D. Because the house was not occupied by anyone.
4. From the second paragraph, we know that _____.
   A. the house was in good condition except for the kitchen ceiling damaged by rain water
   B. the house was not so dirty as they had expected
   C. they would rather not rent the house
   D. they had to have the floors repaired
5. Which of the following is TRUE?
   A. The walls were badly damaged.
   B. The landlord asked the couple to repair the kitchen.
   C. The couple had to pay one month's rent as a deposit.
   D. There were several pictures hanging in one room.

Task 2

Directions: *Read the following diagram or picture and make the correct choice.*

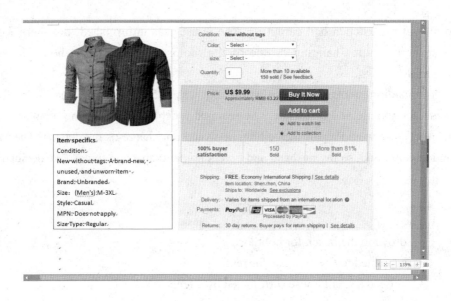

6. How many pieces of the shirt are in stock?
   A. 150. B. More than 81%.
   C. At least 10. D. 100.
7. Where is the place of shipment?
   A. U.S.A. B. Shenzhen, China.
   C. Worldwide. D. See details.
8. What is the style of the men's shirts?
   A. Casual. B. Fashionable.
   C. Slim fit. D. Comfort.
9. What is the condition of the items?
   A. With new tags. B. A famous brand.
   C. Brand-new. D. All sizes.
10. If you want to return your item, you should _____.
    A. return it within 7 days B. pay for the return shipping
    C. return it after a month D. call the seller to solve the problem

Task 3

Directions: *Read the following passage. After reading it, you should complete the information by filling in the blanks **in no more than three words** in the table below.*

To: All managers and Department Heads
Subject: New Communication Training Program
Clear, friendly, efficient communication skills are essential for building

relationships with your customers. You can use it for the benefit of your business. A new online training program is available on the LearnWell website. It will help Company employees create "customer-friendly" communication.

Please visit the website for a memo from the organizer. The memo provides a general view of this customer-friendly communication training program. It also explains how employees can register for the online training. Please forward this e-mail to your employees and encourage them to sign up for training at their leisure time as soon as possible.

Thank you for your support as we work to improve your employees' customer communication in their business activities.

MEMO

To: All managers and Department Heads
Subject: New ___11___ for employees
Training Program:
    1) **Type of training:** a new ___12___ training program on the LearnWell website.
    2) **Skills to train:** clear, ___13___ and efficient communication
    3) **Purpose of training:** to help the employees to create ___14___ communication
    Way of Registration: visit ___15___ for a memo from the organizer

---

Task 4

Directions: *The following is a list of terms. After reading it, you are required to find those items given in Chinese in the table below. Then you should put the corresponding letters in the brackets.*

A—Cash Settlement	I—Trade Volume
B—Price Regulation	J—Credit Transaction
C—Trade Deficit	K—Trade Surplus
D—Import/export Quota	L—Preferential Policies
E—Tariff Free	M—Cash on Delivery
F—Payment by Installments	N—Special Discount
G—Retail Price	O—Wholesale Price
H—Transit Trade	

Example: （ C ）贸易逆差　　　　　（ L ）优惠政策
16. （　）转口贸易　　　　　（　）分期付款
17. （　）贸易逆差　　　　　（　）进/出口限额
18. （　）赊账交易　　　　　（　）免税
19. （　）现金结算　　　　　（　）批发价
20. （　）交货付款　　　　　（　）特殊折扣

Task 5

Directions: *Read the following passage. After reading it, you are required to complete the answers that follow the questions. You should write your answers* ***in no more than three words.***

Resume of Lin Tao

Address:	No.188 Zhong Guancun Road, Beijing EXACT Trading Co. Ltd. Beijing 100080
Position Sought:	Computer Engineer with Taixing Data Engineering Co. Ltd.
Qualifications:	Five years' work experience in operating computers
Professional Experience:	1. Computer Engineering, EXACT Trading Co. Ltd. from 2013 to date 2. Operate flow-charts, update methods of operation 3. Adept (擅长) at operating IBM-PCs
Education:	1. Tsinghua University, 2009–2013, B.S.in Computer Science 2. Beijing No.101 Middle School, 2002–2009
Course included:	1. Computer Science　　　2. Systems Design and Analysis 3. PASCAL Programming　4. Operating System 5. COBOL Programming　 6. D-BASE Programming 7. FORTRAN Programming 8. Systems Management
English Proficiency:	Fluent in listening, speaking, reading and writing
Hobbies:	Swimming
Personal Data:	**Born:** May 19,1988　　**Height:** 182 cm **Health:** Excellent　　　**Weight:** 70 kg **Marital Status:** Single
References:	Will be supplied upon request

21. What kind of job does he apply for?

　　He applies for _____.

22. Which part of the computer technology is he skilled in?

　　He is skilled in _____.

23. How many programming courses has he learned?

   He has learned _____.

24. How about his foreign language?

   His English is _____.

25. According to the last line, what does the writer mean?

   He means that he will supply some references if _____.

Part Ⅲ Translation (English into Chinese)

1. The problem of how human speech began is one which men will never stop exploring.

   A. 人类从来不会停止寻找人类语言是怎么起源的。

   B. 对于人类语言是怎么开始的这个问题，人类的探索永远不会停歇。

   C. 人类语言是怎样起源的，这是人们永远也不会停止探索的问题。

2. Peace and development are the main themes of the times, an era full of both hope and challenges.

   A. 和平与发展是充满了时代希望和挑战的主题。

   B. 和平与发展是既充满着希望又充满着挑战的现时代的主题。

   C. 和平与发展是现时代的主题，这个时代既充满了希望，也充满着挑战。

3. If you are buying a car, you may pay for it with your savings.

   A. 假使你正在买一辆汽车，你也许会透支购买。

   B. 如果你要买一辆汽车，你可以用自己的储蓄存款支付。

   C. 假定你打算买一辆汽车，你得花掉你的部分存款。

4. It is undoubtedly true that poverty is still a problem in this country, as is the case in many other developing and even developed economies.

   A. 贫困毫无疑问仍然是这个国家面临的一个问题,正如其他许多发展中乃至发达的经济体制一样。

   B. 正如其他许多发展中的经济体制乃至发达的经济体制一样,贫困无疑仍然是这个国家的一个问题。

   C. 毫无疑问，这个国家同其他许多发展中国家乃至发达国家一样，仍存在贫困问题。

5. This is to certify that the patient, Mr. Tomas, male, aged 41, was admitted into our hospital on June 9, 2000, for suffering from acute appendicitis (急性阑尾炎). After immediate operation and ten days of treatment, he has got complete recovery and will be discharged on June 19, 2000. It is suggested that he rest for one week at home before resuming his work.

Part Ⅳ Practical Writing

Directions: *This part is to test your ability to do practical writing. You are required to write a lost and found announcement according to the information given below in Chinese. Remember to do your writing on the Translation/Composition Sheet.*

说明：根据下列信息，写一张失物招领布告。

失 物 招 领

有人在商场内捡到手表一只，交至本室。丢表者请带身份证前来认领，特此布告。

失物招领办公室

Words for reference: 商场 shopping center 手表 wrist watch 认领 claim

Supplementary Reading

Passage A

It Was Over 阳光总在风雨后

Middle School. For three long, hard years those two words meant only one thing to me: torture. It all started during my first week of school when I started taking the bus. My family was too poor to afford a car at the time, so that was my only way to get there without having to walk two and a half miles. As soon as I got onto the bus, things were different. The kids were acting like jerks!

Halfway to school, the kids had already started picking on the special needs kids who had been mainstreamed that year. They had already made fun of their looks and their weight when I couldn't take it anymore. I looked at David, the leader of the bullies, and said, "Hey! Shut up! How would you feel if someone did that to you?"

At that moment, I felt like I was on top of the world. The kids who were being picked on looked at me as if I were their hero. Even the bus driver stopped the bus to look at me. I thought that I had stopped the teasing when suddenly David looked at me with a mean smirk. "I don't know," he said, "How does it feel, FATTY?" That was when I became the center of their torment.

中学——在那漫长而艰难的三年之中，这个词对我来说只是意味着"痛苦"。那一切都是从我乘坐校车上学的第一周开始的。那时我家很穷，根本买不起车，因此若想不必步行两英里半去上学，乘坐校车就成为我唯一的交通方式。当我一上车，情况就有了变化。一些孩子表现得就像混蛋一样。

车至中途，"小霸王"们就开始捉弄起那一年和普通学生在一起上学的需要特殊教育的孩子们。他们嘲笑那些孩子们的长相和体重使我实在忍无可忍。我看了看大卫——这群"小霸王"的头儿，说道："喂，闭嘴！如果别人这样说你，你会有什么感受呢？"

就在那一刻，我感觉自己无比伟大。那些一直被捉弄的孩子们看着我，仿佛我是他们眼中的英雄。甚至连司机也停下车回头看我。我本以为已经制止了"小霸王"们的"恶行"，突然大卫看着我，脸上挂着卑鄙的坏笑。"我可不知道，"他说："你感觉怎么样啊，胖猪？"随即我便成了他们戏弄的主角。

Every day when I got on the bus, I had to deal with them. I had gum stuck in my hair, food thrown at me, and I was called the cruelest and most disgusting names. Sometimes, the bullies would even take my backpack from me and throw it outside. They would watch me run after it from the windows. As a result of all the bullying, my grades suffered terribly. I went from having all As and Bs, to having Ds and Fs. I was miserable. All I wanted to do was go back to elementary school where I felt safe and happy.

When my mom finally bought a car, and was able to drive me to school, I thought that things were going to get better. I was wrong. I had become the bullies' little pet. They made fun of me every day in the hallway. They would wait for me to do something that they could tease me for. I had practically no friends because nobody wanted to hang out with the butt of everyone's teasing. I was all alone. I felt as if I were holding the weight of the world on my shoulders.

During this lonely period, I started writing. I would write horror novels and sequels and prequels to books that I had read. It was my only form of escape. One day, in Language Arts class, our assignment was to write a dragon slayer novel. Just when I was about done writing my story, the kid who sat next to me grabbed it and started to read it. I half expected him to tear it up when he looked at me and said, "Hey, this is pretty good! My name is Ricky. You're

此后，每天乘车，我都不得不与他们纠缠。他们把口香糖粘在我的头发上，把食物抛向我，还用最恶毒、最恶心的名字辱骂我。有时，他们甚至把我的书包抢走扔出窗外。而他们则透过车窗看着我冲出去捡回书包。由于受到这些"小霸王"们的欺侮，我的成绩一落千丈。从起初全部A等、B等一路降到D等甚至是F等。我非常痛苦。真想重新回到小学，在那里我能感受到安全与快乐。

等我的妈妈终于买了私家车，可以送我去上学，我想一切都会变得好起来的。而事实上我错了。我已经成为那些"小霸王"们的"玩物"。他们每天都在走廊里取笑我。他们总是等在那里，观察我，然后拿我寻开心。实际上我几乎没有什么朋友，因为没人愿意与我这个众人取笑对象混在一起。我总是独来独往。我感觉自己仿佛肩负着整个世界的重量。

就在那段孤独的日子里，我开始练习写作。我喜欢写恐怖小说以及给我以前读过的书写前传或续篇。有一天，在语言艺术课上，老师让我们写一篇关于屠龙者的小说。在我就要写完的时候，坐在我旁边的同学一把抢了过去，开始看了起来。我忐忑不安，以为他会把我的文章撕得粉碎。但是他却抬起头看了看我，说道："嗨，故事真棒！我叫瑞奇。你叫詹妮弗，

Jennifer, right?"

When Ricky said those words, he made me one of the happiest people in the room. That day, I felt like I was walking on sunshine. I had lunch with him and his friends that day. We talked about our favorite horror movies, books, and the math teacher that all of the sixth graders thought was evil. We also talked about the bullies. We all bonded together over how hurt we were by them. Somehow, we all understood each other. We could joke around and be ourselves and not try to fit in.

After a whole long year of torment, I felt wanted. I was no longer being teased. It was finally over.

对吧？"

瑞奇的话使我感到自己成为教室里最快乐的人之一。那天，我感觉好像一直走在阳光里。我和他以及他的朋友们共进午餐。一起谈论我们最喜爱的恐怖电影、图书，还有所有六年级学生都极不喜欢的数学老师。我们也谈到了那些"小霸王"们。他们给我们带来的伤害大家都感同身受。好在我们彼此理解，我们互相开玩笑，展示真实的自我，而不必去迎合他人。

历经了整整一年的苦闷，我终于被人接受了。我不再被人取笑。最终一切都过去了。

Passage B

Learning of Value 价值的真谛

I saw something a bit disturbing last week. I had to stop at a drugstore to pick something up, and while there I saw a kid about thirteen years up buy a Monster drink, about 24 ounces of caffeine fix. That in itself saddened me, to think that this kid has been seduced by marketers and peers to think that a caffeine fix is a positive thing in life. I was shocked, though, to see the price affixed to the can: $3.49. This kid was spending more on one drink than anyone making minimum wage earns in half an hour of work—and I feel taken when I have to pay $1.19 for a large soda at a gas station when I'm

上周我看到了一件令我有点烦心的事情。那天我因故不得已在一家杂货店前停车去买点东西。在那儿，我遇见一个十三四岁的小孩买了一听含有咖啡因成分的约 24 盎司重的"怪物能量"饮料。这个孩子在推销员及同龄人的误导下竟然认为咖啡因成分是日常生活中的有益物质，一想到这件事情本身便令我很难过。不过当我看到贴在罐体上的3.49美元的价格时，我更为震惊。因为这个孩子在一罐饮料上的花销超过了任何人半个小时的最低工资。对我来说，外出旅行

traveling. I couldn't help but think that this kid never had been taught of the value of money, and of the concept of exchanging the money for something of comparable value.

I see this principal all over as I go through my day. I see rims on car wheels that cost upwards of $500, just for a little bit of decoration on a vehicle. I see people spend four or five dollars for a cup of coffee, hundreds of dollars for cell phones that they almost never use, thousands of dollars on huge television sets that they almost never watch. All around us are ads and commercials that keep us wanting to buy things that keep us dissatisfied with the way things are, and those ads and commercials are trying to convince us that if we just buy some more stuff—no matter what the cost— we'll be happier and more content.

But somewhere along the line we have to learn to make our own decisions about value. There's a common law of economics that states that many poor people will stay poor because of the decisions that they make about how to spend their money. How many people have you known or known of, for example, who have little money yet who buy a very expensive car with high monthly payments? And how many people are in trouble right now because they bought houses that were more expensive than they could afford?

While I wouldn't say that the answer to

时，在加油站花费1.19美元的买一大瓶汽水都觉得是被宰了。我不由得想到肯定从未有人曾向这个孩子灌输金钱的价值以及应该用金钱来换取物有所值商品的观念。

每一天，我都能看到这样的事情发生。我看到人们仅仅是为了少许的装饰效果就花费500多美元为车辆装上轮箍。我看到有些人花费四五美元购买一杯咖啡，或是花费数百美元购买一部他们极少使用的手机，甚至花费几千美元购买他们几乎从不观看的大屏幕电视机。我们的周围充斥着形形色色的广告使我们总是喜新厌旧，不断购买一些新的物品。那些广告试图让我们相信无论花费多少，只要买得越多，我们便会感到更加快乐，更加满足。

但是在某些方面我们必须学会始终由自己来对价值做出决策。一项通用经济学法则表明，许多穷人之所以持续贫困是由于他们所做出的消费决策所导致的。例如，你认识或是听说过有多少人自己没多少钱却买了高月供的极其昂贵的轿车？还有多少人因为买了超过其支付能力的高价房子而眼下正陷入困境，不能自拔？

然而我并不是说正确的金钱

our money issues would be to skimp and save every penny and never have any fun in life, it is important that we learn about value and about when to spend how much. A few years ago, for example, my wife and I had cell phones. At the time I worked half an hour from home, I was on the road with sports teams a lot, and my wife also was on the road quite a bit. The cell phones made sense, even though we didn't use them much—at least we knew that if anything happened, we could contact one another.

Then we moved someplace where we didn't need the phones any more, for we both worked close to one another and we weren't on the road much. Suddenly, the $75 every month to keep the phones made no sense, so we got rid of them. They were now just a luxury item, no longer as necessary as they were before. They simply didn't have the same value that they had had before. And even though it had been quite convenient to make an occasional phone call from wherever I happened to be, that convenience was no longer worth the amount of money we would have had to pay to maintain it.

It's unfortunate that money is such a huge part of our lives, and that it affects our lives so very strongly. But that's the way things are, so the best that we can do is learn to define the value of our money for ourselves and to exchange our money for goods and services that have equal or even greater value. While a woman I know who is broke can go out and spend almost a

观就是要做吝啬鬼，节省每一分钱，从而导致生活毫无乐趣可言。重要的是我们要懂得物有所值以及何时应该花费多少。例如，几年前，我和妻子都有手机。那时我的工作地点离家有半个小时的路程，我总是随运动队东奔西走，而我的妻子也经常出差在外。手机不可或缺，尽管我们不是经常使用，但至少我们清楚如果有事，我们可以相互联系。

后来我们搬了家，不再需要手机了。因为我们的工作地点离得很近，而且我们不再经常出差了。这样一来，每月75美元的手机费用就变得毫无意义了，因此我们就弃之不用了。如今它们对我们来说就成为一种奢侈品，不再像以前那般必要了。就它们的使用价值来说已经今非昔比了。尽管我可以偶尔用它很方便地随时随地打个电话，但这种便利与我必须支付的手机费用相比，实在不值。

不幸的是，金钱在我们的日常生活中是如此的举足轻重，从而极大地影响了我们的生活。不过现实生活就是如此。因此，我们的最佳做法就是学会为自己定义金钱的价值，并且使所交换到的商品与服务物有所值甚至物超所值。不过我认识一位妇女已经破产却花费近百美元做头发。我想她无法负担，

hundred dollars on a new hairdo, I know that she really can't afford it, and that its value is not nearly as much as she thinks it is. When my wife and I go on vacation in a few weeks and spend $400 on a hotel room in Yosemite National Park, though—which is much more than we've ever spent on a hotel room before—we both have considered the cost, the location, and the reasons for our vacation, and we both agree that there is great value in the price that we'll pay.

Money is here, and it's a part of our lives. We can live with it and have it work for us, or we can squander it and lose it and become angry and frustrated with our loss. The choice is ours, but one thing is for sure—the path to happiness doesn't lie in exchanging our money for goods or services of little value; rather, we need to make sure that the money we spend is money well spent. Only then can we avoid the resentment and frustration that will come over having wasted money when we didn't need to.

而且它的价值远不及她自己认为的那样。几周后我和妻子将要去度假，准备入住尤塞米提国家公园内每晚400美元的酒店房间。尽管价格比我们以前所住过的任何酒店房间都要昂贵，但是我们通盘考虑了住宿开支、酒店位置以及度假的初衷，因此我们一致认为我们要付的价格绝对物有所值。

金钱就在身边，成为我们生活中的一部分。我们可以依靠它生活，让它为我们服务。我们也可以挥霍金钱，最终一无所有，导致我们因此而愤怒异常，倍感失落。选择权在我们自己手里，但是有一点可以肯定，幸福的感觉不会因用我们的金钱交换了那些毫无价值的商品或服务而存在，而是我们需要确信我们所花费的每一分钱都物有所值。只有那样我们才能避免因为不必要的花销浪费金钱而产生的怨恨与沮丧。

Unit Two

Part I Vocabulary & Structure

Section A

Directions: *In this section, there are 10 incomplete sentences. You are required to complete each one by deciding on the most appropriate word or words from the 4 choices marked A, B, C and D. Then you should mark the corresponding letter on the Answer Sheet with a single line through the center.*

1. Their talks next week are expected to focus _____ business management.
   A. on   B. with   C. in   D. of

2. There are no openings at present, so the company will not _____ anybody.
   A. handle   B. lead   C. hire   D. dismiss

3. I wanted to know when and where we should _____ our assignments.
   A. set back   B. fall into   C. take off   D. hand in

4. We considered _____ to California at first, but decided not to in the end.
   A. move   B. moving   C. to move   D. moved

5. Australia has its own _____ identity, which is very different from that of Britain.
   A. busy   B. central   C. capable   D. cultural

6. The internet allows rural school children _____ about what is happening in the world.
   A. to learn   B. learning   C. learn   D. learned

7. The grocery store has been closed down since no one wanted to _____ the business.
   A. put up   B. give off   C. take over D. bring about

8. The CEO said that it would never be _____ late to apologize for its poor service.
   A. much   B. too   C. so   D. very

9. The president gave a detailed _____ of his proposal at the meeting.
   A. explanation B. search   C. balance   D. word

10. Last year the employees in our department were so busy _____ they were

not able to take a vacation.

  A. which B. what C. who D. that

Section B

Directions: *There are 5 incomplete statements here. You should fill in each blank with the proper form of the word given in brackets. Write the word or words in the corresponding space on the Answer Sheet.*

 11. (Surprising) _____, the team was able to finish the task two weeks ahead of schedule.

 12. The designers from our firm are ready (assist) _____ you throughout the whole process.

 13. It seems to me that his solution is much (effective) _____ than mine.

 14. Your strong determination to improve services has left a deep (impress) _____ on us.

 15. We are pleased to have you visit us and look forward to (meet) _____ you next week.

Part II Reading Comprehension

Directions: *This part is to test your reading abilities. There are 5 tasks for you to fulfill. You should read the materials carefully and do the tasks as you are instructed.*

Task 1

Directions: *Reading the passage and make the correct choice.*

 Specialists in marketing have studied how to make people buy more food in a supermarket. They do all kinds of things that you do not even notice. For example, the simple, ordinary food that everybody must buy, like bread, milk, flour and vegetable oil, is spread all over the store. You have to walk by all the more interesting—and more expensive—things in order to find what you need. The expensive food is in packages with bright colored pictures. This food is placed at eye level so you see it and want to buy it. The things that you have to buy anyway are usually located on a higher or lower shelves. One study showed that when a supermarket moved four products from floor to eye level, it sold 78 percent more.

 Another study showed that for every minute a person is in a supermarket after the first half hour, she or he spends 50 cents. If someone stays forty minutes, the supermarket has an additional $5. So the store has a comfortable temperature in summer and winter, and it plays soft music. It is a pleasant place for people to stay—and spend more money.

Some stores have red or pink lights over the meat so the meat looks redder. They put light green paper around lettuce and put apples in red plastic bags.

So be careful in the supermarket. You may go home with a bag of food you were not planning to buy. The supermarket, not you, decided you should buy it.

1. Marketing specialists study _____.
   A. plants suitable for human needs
   B. how to build shelves
   C. method of selling more products
   D. how to own supermarket

2. The more expensive kind of food is _____.
   A. in bright colored packages
   B. on higher shelves
   C. all near the front of the store
   D. on lower shelves

3. According to the selecting, children's books are probably _____.
   A. on low shelves
   B. on high shelves
   C. spread all over the store
   D. sold in supermarket

4. A supermarket plays soft music because _____.
   A. people like to listen to it
   B. the store has a comfortable temperature
   C. it will make people spend more money
   D. it will remind people to buy the things they want

5. A good way to save money in a supermarket is to _____.
   A. go just before dinner
   B. buy things that are in the prettiest packages
   C. walk around and see what you need
   D. make a list of what you need before you go

Task 2

Directions: *Read the following diagram or picture and make the correct choice.*

Your mouth is in for a treat. Metromint is pure water infused with real mint that cools and refreshes with every sip. And the rest of your body will like it, too. Metromint is all natural. It contains no sugar, no preservatives, and no sweeteners. And that means zero calories. So, you can refresh to your heart's content, 100% guilt-free.

Find us at your favorite grocer or online at **metromint.com**.

6. The advertisement above is about _____.
   A. a kind of food   B. a kind of drink
   C. a kind of water   D. a kind of lipsticks
7. The commodity advertised contains _____.
   A. sugar   B. preservatives
   C. sweeteners   D. real mint
8. It can make you feel _____.
   A. cool and refresh   B. sweet
   C. pure and simple   D. terrible
9. From the picture we can know that there are _____ choices available for this commodity.
   A. 2   B. 3   C. 4   D. 5
10. If you want to know something or buy the commodity you can _____.
    A. go to ask your friends   B. go to grocery stores
    C. go to school   D. go to the library

Task 3

Directions: *Read the following passage. After reading it, you should complete the information by filling in the blanks **in no more than three words** in the table below.*

A: Do all American students live on campus?

B: No. It is up to your own preference: on campus or off campus.

A: Do American male and female college students live in the same dormitory buildings on campus?

B: Usually they live in the same building but on different floors. After midnight the opposite gender must return to their own rooms. At my university, there is still an all-girls building.

A: How does a student get the renting information about off-campus living?

B: Almost anywhere. They can find renting information in the university newspaper, the local newspaper, the dining services and from their friends and classmates. The following is a sample from a classified advertising section of a local newspaper.

For Rent
Lease Now to July
2 bedroom unfurnished apartment with garage. Close to Campus
Stove, refrig, dishwasher, 1-car garage.
Trash & water paid.

> Two adults $250 each per month.
> 955 4th Street. Call 348-7746.

A: What is the important information people need to mention?
B: "Unfurnished" means you need to buy some dresser（梳妆台）, table, and mattress（床垫）

---

11. Whether American students live on campus or not is up to _____.

12. American students can find renting information in the _____ newspaper.

13. That you need to buy some dresser, table, and mattress means the apartment is _____.

14. If college students who live in the same dormitory building are all male rather than female, we call this building _____.

15. If two students rent the apartment mentioned in the ad., they need not pay for _____.

Task 4

Directions: *The following is a list of terms. After reading it, you are required to find those items given in Chinese in the table below. Then you should put the corresponding letters in the brackets.*

A—General Manager
B—Human Resource Manager
C—Production Manager
D—Technology Manager
E—Secretary
F—Department Manager
G—Company Manager
H—Sales Manager
I—Financial Manager
J—Accountant
K—Sales Representative
L—Purchasing Department
M—Account Manager
N—Product Supervisor
O—Support Service
P—Technical Clerk
Q—Product Research and Development

Example: （ C ）生产部经理　　　　（ E ）秘书
16. （　）人事部经理　　　　（　）财务部经理
17. （　）会计　　　　　　　（　）产品主管
18. （　）客户经理　　　　　（　）采购部
19. （　）产品研发　　　　　（　）后勤服务
20. （　）总经理　　　　　　（　）销售部经理

Task 5

Directions: *Read the following passage. After reading it, you are required to complete the answers that follow the questions. You should write your answers **in no more than three words**.*

Meeting Minutes

Present: The Red. A.C. Hills, in the chair.
　　　　　Miss Kwan Yung Kit,
　　　　　Mr. K.L. Liang,　　　　　Mr. John Lim,
　　　　　Mr. John Luke,　　　　　Mr. Owen Mak
　　　　　Mr. C.Y. Ching, Secretary

Apologies for Absence were received from: Miss Maria Wongs

1. The minutes of the meeting of the Executive Committee held on Monday, February 11, 2012, were read and approved.

2. Matters Arising from the Minutes

The Secretary reported that Miss Elizabeth Tsin has accepted the post of Public Relations Officer and will assume her duties on March 1, 2012.

3. Social Convener（会议召集人）

A number of social gatherings will be organized in the near future, so it is necessary to co-opt（指定）a Social Convener into the committee. After considering the choice in detail, it was agreed that Miss Susan Young be the Social Convener.

4. Fund-Raising Campaign

After a detailed discussion, it was unanimously（一致地）agreed that the Association will launch a fund-raising campaign in August, with a target of twenty thousand dollars.

5. Any Other Business

The Secretary reported that NCR has donated one hundred books to the Association. The Chairman would write a letter to thank the company on behalf of the Association.

6. Date and Place of the Next Meeting

The Chairman announced that the next meeting of the Committee will be held at 6 a.m. on Friday, March 15, 2012, in the Conference Room.

7. There being no other business to discuss, the meeting was closed at 7:30 p.m.

　　　　　　　　　　　　　　　　　　　　　　Signature (Secretary)
　　　　　　　　　　　　　　　　　　　　　　Signature (Chairman)

21. Who was absent from the meeting?

_____.

22. What post has Miss Elizabeth Tsin accepted?

   Miss Elizabeth Tsin has accepted the post of _____.

23. Why would the chairman write a letter to thank NCR on behalf of the Association?

   The Chairman would write a letter to thank NCR because it has _____ to the Association.

24. What is the target of the fund-raising campaign?

   The target for the campaign is _____.

25. What activity was Miss Susan Young supposed to do in the near future?

   She was appointed Social Convener to organize _____.

Part Ⅲ   Translation (English into Chinese)

1. For safety, all passengers are required to review this card and follow these instructions when needed.

   A. 为了安全，请各位乘客反复阅读本卡片，务必按照各项规定执行。

   B. 为了安全，要求所有乘客仔细阅读本卡片各项内容，必要时照其执行。

   C. 为了保险起见，要求所有乘客在需要时都能看到这张卡片及以下这些内容。

2. People now have more leisure time, which is the reason why the demand for services has increased so rapidly.

   A. 如今人们有更多的时间去娱乐，从而影响了劳务资源的快速上升。

   B. 如今希望有时间娱乐的人越来越多，这是因为服务质量迅速提高了。

   C. 如今人们有更多的闲暇时间，因而对各种服务的需求增长如此快。

3. Passengers going to the airport by arranged buses must take the bus at the time and places as shown before.

   A. 搭乘专车去往机场的旅客，务必在下列指定的时间和地点乘车。

   B. 搭乘公共汽车去机场的旅客必须乘这班车，时间和地点安排如下。

   C. 经安排搭乘汽车去机场的旅客，应按规定的时间和地点乘车。

4. Mr. Smith has canceled his trip because an urgent matter has come up which requires his immediate attention.

   A. 史密斯先生推迟了旅行，因为发生了一件大家都十分关注的突发事件。

   B. 史密斯先生取消了旅行，因为发生了一件紧急的事情需要他立即处理。

   C. 史密斯先生取消了旅行，因为有一件棘手的事情需要他予以密切关注。

5. Thank you for choosing our restaurant during your visit to London. Services to guests of the restaurant are a large part of our tasks, and we are grateful for the opportunity to serve you. We would like to invite your comments on our performance and to learn from your experiences. Please take a few moments to complete our customer response form so that we may serve you better in the future.

Part Ⅳ   Practical Writing

Directions: *This part is to test your ability to do practical writing. You are required to write a letter of thanks according to the information given below in Chinese. Remember to do your writing on the Translation/Composition Sheet.*

说明：假定你是 JKM 公司的 Thomas Black，刚从巴黎出差回来，请给在巴黎的 Jane Costa 小姐写一封感谢信。（注意：必须包括对收信人的称呼、写信日期、发信人的签名等基本格式）

写信日期：2008 年 12 月 21 日

内容：

1）感谢她在巴黎期间的热情接待；

2）告诉她巴黎给你留下了美好的印象，你非常喜欢法国的……，参观工厂和学校后学到了很多……；

3）期待再次与她见面。

Supplementary Reading

Passage A

A Miracle of Tears   眼泪的奇迹

| It was one of the hottest days of the dry | 那是干旱季节里最热的一 |

season. We had not seen rain in almost a month. The crops were dying. Cows had stopped giving milk. The creeks and streams were long gone back into the earth. It was a dry season that would bankrupt several farmers before it was through.

Every day, my husband and his brothers would go about the arduous process of trying to get water to the fields.

Lately this process had involved taking a truck to the local water rendering plant and filling it up with water. But severe rationing had cut everyone off. If we didn't see some rain soon...we would lose everything.

It was on this day that I learned the true lesson of sharing and witnessed the only miracle I have seen with my own eyes.

I was in the kitchen making lunch for my husband and his brothers when I saw my six-year-old son, Billy, walking toward the woods. He wasn't walking with the usual carefree abandon of a youth but with a serious purpose. I could only see his back.

He was obviously walking with a great effort... trying to be as still as possible.

Minutes after he disappeared into the woods, he came running out again, toward the house. I went back to making sandwiches; thinking that whatever task he had been doing was completed.

Moments later, however, he was once again walking in that slow purposeful stride toward the

天，我们几乎有一个月没有看到下雨了，庄稼就要枯死了。奶牛也不再产奶。大小河流都早已干涸。这样的干旱季节在它结束之前就将使部分农民破产。

每一天，我的丈夫都与他的兄弟们一起不辞辛苦地去取水浇灌田地。

近来，他们动用了卡车到当地的供水厂装水。但严格的限量供应却使他们难以如愿。如果再不下雨，我们将失去一切。

就在那一天，我上了关于分享的真正一课，并亲眼看见了从未见过的一次奇迹。

当时我正在厨房为丈夫和他的兄弟们准备午饭，突然看见六岁的儿子——比利，正向小树林走去。看上去，他不像往常那般无忧无虑、信马由缰，而是郑重其事，目标明确。我只能看到他的背影。
很明显，他努力前行，尽可能做到悄无声息。

几分钟后，他便消失在树林里。很快他又跑出树林，奔向家中。我继续做着三明治，暗自寻思不知比利刚刚完成了一件什么"秘密任务"。

然而，片刻之后，他又迈着缓慢而坚定的步伐向树林走去。这

23

woods. This activity went on for an hour: walk carefully to the woods, run back to the house. Finally I couldn't take it any longer and I crept out of the house and followed him on his journey (being very careful not to be seen...as he was obviously doing important work and didn't need his Mommy checking up on him).

He was cupping both hands in front of him as he walked, being very careful not to spill the water he held in them. Maybe two or three tablespoons were held in his tiny hands. I sneaked close as he went into the woods.

Branches and thorns slapped his little face, but he did not try to avoid them.

As I leaned in to spy on him, I saw the most amazing site. Several large deer loomed in front of him. Billy walked right up to them. I almost screamed for him to get away.

A huge buck with elaborate antlers was dangerously close. But the buck did not threaten him. He didn't even move as Billy knelt down. And I saw a tiny fawn laying on the ground, obviously suffering from dehydration and heat exhaustion, lift its head with great effort to lap up the water cupped in my beautiful boy's hand.

When the water was gone, Billy jumped up to run back to the house and I hid behind a tree. I followed him back to the house to a spigot to which we had shut off the water. Billy opened it all the way up and a small

样的举动持续了一个小时。小心翼翼地走进树林，然后飞跑回家。最后，我实在忍不住了，蹑手蹑脚地走出家门，跟着比利向前走去（非常小心，以免被他发现。因为，显而易见，他正在做一项重要的事情，不需要妈妈参与其中）。

他把双手在胸前合拢成杯状，慢慢地走着，非常小心，生怕手里捧着的水洒出来。看上去他手捧的水也有两三勺。等他走进树林，我也悄悄靠近。

树枝和荆棘不时刮蹭他的小脸蛋，但是他并不刻意躲闪。

当我探身窥探他的举动时，我看到了令人瞠目结舌的一幕。在他前面隐约可见几只体型硕大的梅花鹿。比利径直走过去。我几乎要尖叫起来，提醒他离开。

一只长着美丽鹿角的壮硕雄鹿近在咫尺，十分危险。但是雄鹿并未对他造成威胁。当比利跪下来的时候，雄鹿竟然一动也不动。我看到一只小鹿正躺在地上，很明显是由于脱水以及高温虚脱导致的。它吃力地抬起头，舔着这个善良男孩手里捧着的那点水。

当水刚被舔干，比利便跳起身，向家跑去。我躲在一棵树后，紧随他返回家中来到一个早就关闭的龙头旁。比利把水阀开到最大，一小滴水缓缓掉了下来。他

trickle began to creep out. He knelt there, letting the drip, drip slowly fill up his makeshift "cup," as the sun beat down on his little back. And it came clear to me: The trouble he had gotten into for playing with the hose the week before. The lecture he had received about the importance of not wasting water. The reason he didn't ask me to help him.

It took almost twenty minutes for the drops to fill his hands.

When he stood up and began the trek back, I was there in front of him.

His little eyes just filled with tears.

"I'm not wasting," was all he said.

As he began his walk, I joined him with a small pot of water from the kitchen. I let him tend to the fawn. I stayed away. It was his job. I stood on the edge of the woods watching the most beautiful heart I have ever known working so hard to save another life. As the tears that rolled down my face began to hit the ground, they were suddenly joined by other drops...and more drops...and more.

I looked up at the sky. It was as if God himself was weeping with pride.

Some will probably say that this was all just a huge coincidence. That miracles don't really exist. That it was bound to rain sometime. And I can't argue with that...I'm not going to try. All I can say is that the rain

跪在那儿，让水滴慢慢装满他用双手临时捧成的"杯子"。此时，强烈的阳光直射到他瘦小的后背上。一下子我全都明白了。为何一周前他在这儿摆弄水管而惹了麻烦。还因此受到了绝不能浪费水的教育以及他不向我求助的原因。

几乎过了20多分钟，水才滴满他的小手。

当他站起来，吃力地回转身，发现我正站在他的前面。

他的双眼立即盈满了泪水。

"我不是在浪费水。"说完他便一言不发。

当比利迈步向前走去的时候，我也从厨房提了一壶水随他前往。我离得远远的，听凭他自己照顾小鹿。那是他的工作。我站在林边注视着我所见过的最美丽的心灵正辛勤忙碌着挽救另外一个生命。泪水从我的脸上滚落，掉到地上。这时我突然发现还有别的水滴也一同掉落，而且越来越多。

我抬头仰望天空。仿佛是上天也为他感到自豪而激动落泪。

有人可能会说那纯粹是一个天大的巧合。那种奇迹根本不存在。那肯定是赶上下雨的时候了。而我不想为此而争辩，我也不会去争辩。我能说的只是那天下的雨挽救了我

that came that day saved our farm...just like the actions of one little boy saved another.

们的农场，正像一个小男孩的行动拯救了另外一个小生命一样。

Passage B

Bad Parking　不文明停车引发的思考

My wife and I were walking through the parking lot at the supermarket the other day when we noticed one of those huge pick-up trucks that almost no one in the world really needs, parked a good foot and a half into the next parking space. There was plenty of room in its own space, but the driver had chosen to park very poorly and make sure that no one could use the space next to theirs.

不久前的一天，正当我和妻子走过超市停车场的时候，我们突然注意到有一辆这世界上几乎没有人真正用得上的大型皮卡车，它停放的位置占用了旁边的车位整整一英尺半以上。原本这辆车的车位上还有足够的空当，但是这位司机却选择如此糟糕的停车方式，为的是确保没有人能够使用旁边的车位。

"It takes all kinds," was my first response, because I've spent years trying to get past a lot of the judgmental tendencies that I was taught while I was young. "What a shame that people have to do things like that," my wife offered.

"真是什么人都有。"这是我的第一反应。尽管多年以来我一直在试图超越小时候所接受的判断取向教育。"人们竟然做出那样的事，真是丢人。"我妻子提出了自己的意见。

I stopped and thought about it for a few seconds, then looked around at the rest of the parking lot. There were a good five hundred cars in it at that hour, and from the looks of it, 99% of them were parked well—their drivers had shown the courtesy necessary to park in a way that still allowed other people to park. "Think about it," I said. "Four hundred ninety-nine people have parked well, and one individual parks poorly and we start using the word 'people' to describe the driver." Because the simple truth of the matter is

我停住脚步，思索了片刻。然后环顾停车场周围，看了看其余的停车位。当时停车场里足足有500辆车，表面看来，99%都停得规规矩矩——那些司机们都表现出停车时应该遵守的规矩。通过这种方式，其他车辆就能顺利停放。"想想吧，"我说，"499个人都能文明停车，只有一个人不讲规则。而我们却用'人们'这个词来形容那位司机。"出现这种情况的原因很简单：当我们看到一个人正在做粗鲁无理或令人厌恶的事情时，我们总是忘记成千上万并未做那种粗鲁

that when we see one person doing something rude or obnoxious, we forget about the thousands of people who aren't doing something rude or obnoxious.

When a driver cuts us off in traffic, we tend to be more likely to say "Why do people drive like such idiots?" rather than "Why is this particular person driving so poorly at this particular time?" I've been driving for many years, and the percentage of good drivers FAR outweighs the percentage of poor drivers. "People" don't necessarily drive poorly, but individuals do.

Why is it so easy to generalize negative things to all people, when most people are kind and considerate and thoughtful at least some of the time? I wish I had an answer to that—my guess is that it has something to do with avoiding conflict with individuals, even if the conflict is just in our minds. It could also have to do with our ego's tendency to want to set ourselves apart from everyone else, for that's how the ego thrives, by getting us to focus on how separate we are, how different we are. As with most things, it's probably a combination of many factors.

I do see the results of such thinking, though. It gets quite easy for us to be judgmental and to find things that are "wrong" with others, and the more we do that, the more we put ourselves up on a pedestal that keeps us separate. We're also far less likely to see the positive side of things if

无理或是令人厌恶事情的其他人。

当一位司机在车流中阻碍了我们前行时，我们往往会这样说，"为什么人们会这样傻乎乎地开车？"而不是这样说，"为什么这个人在这个特殊的时段把车开得这么差？"我已经开车多年，想来，好司机的比例要远远超过差司机的比例。事实上，并非"人们"开车不讲规则，而是某些个人所为。

为什么当绝大多数人至少在有些时候与人为善、体贴周到、为他人着想的时候，我们却总是轻易地把否定面归咎于所有人？真希望我能找到这个问题的答案——我猜想这和我们力图避免与个人起冲突有关，即便这种冲突仅存在于我们的想象之中。这也可能与我们的自我倾向性有关，想把自己与他人截然分开；因为这就是自我膨胀的方式，让自己专注于如何特立独行，如何与众不同。就大多数事情而言，很可能是多种因素结合的产物。

但是，我确实看到了如此思考的结果。这样一来，我们很容易就能评判并找出他人"做错"的事情。而且越是这样做，我们就越会把自己置于高位，从而把自己始终与他人隔离开来。如果我们总是关注于消极面，我们就不可能看到事情积极的一面。我

we keep focused on the negative—my wife and I almost didn't notice the many cars that were parked well because the car that was parked poorly captured our attention. Once we fall into this trap, how many of the wonderful things in the world do we miss because we're focused on the things that may not be so wonderful?

Try it sometime—the next time you're out and about, notice how quickly it can affect you when someone cuts in front of you without saying "excuse me." Notice how much longer that negative feeling tends to last than the good feeling that came when someone else did the same thing but excused themselves.

What this comes down to, of course, is a matter of choice. What do we choose to focus on? And if we focus on something negative, does it hinder our view of the positive? Do we lose sight of the beauty and wonder around us because of one individual's actions, even if what that person does definitely is abnormal? Our lives are ours to live, and the way we see our world is up to us. The next time you see someone doing something that seems rude, look around and see how many people aren't doing rude things—you may find out that the rude person truly is an exception, and not really worth the time or effort or energy that we spend thinking about him or her.

和妻子几乎都没有注意到那些文明停放的汽车，是因为那辆没按规则停放的汽车完全吸引了我们的注意力。一旦我们陷入这个误区，由于只是关注那些不怎么美好的东西，那么世界上有多少美好事物会被我们错过呢？

有机会就试一下吧——下次外出闲逛的时候，体会一下如果有人在你前面挡道而不说"抱歉"，它会多快地影响你的情绪。体会一下与当别人做了同样的事情而向你表示歉意所带给你的好感相比，这种消极情绪持续的时间要长多少呢？

当然，这要归结在选择这一点上。我们会选择去关注什么呢？试想，如果我们关注消极的东西，它是否会阻碍我们的积极看法呢？即使某个人的所作所为确实违背常理，我们是否会因为此人的行为而对周围的美景以及奇观视而不见呢？我们的人生靠我们自己去度过，我们看待世界的方式也取决于我们自己。下一次当你看到某人正在做无礼之事的时候，环顾一下周围，看看有多少人没有那样做。——你就会发现那个无礼的人只是一个例外，不值得我们花时间、花力气和花精力去考虑他或者她。

Unit Three

Part I Vocabulary & Structure

Section A

Directions: *In this section, there are 10 incomplete sentences. You are required to complete each one by deciding on the most appropriate word or words from the 4 choices marked A, B, C and D. Then you should mark the corresponding letter on the Answer Sheet with a single line through the center.*

1. When I changed my job, I had to _____ to another apartment.
   A. gather   B. post   C. master   D. move

2. We are looking for a secretary _____ speaks Chinese fluently.
   A. who   B. which   C. whom   D. whose

3. This record will help your safety officer _____ what the problem is.
   A. bring up   B. put on   C. find out   D. take in

4. The more you concentrate on training, _____ the results will be.
   A. good   B. better   C. the better   D. the best

5. This workshop is to cope _____ the challenges we have faced worldwide.
   A. at   B. with   C. of   D. in

6. The traditional stores have found it difficult to _____ with online shops recently.
   A. argue   B. begin   C. meet   D. compete

7. According to the report, the local economy had _____ rapid growth over that period.
   A. practiced   B. experienced C. controlled   D. connected

8. _____ the website in Chinese, there is an English version provided.
   A. In addition to   B. On behalf of
   C. As a result of   D. For the purpose of

9. Last year some additional measures _____ to protect customers' personal information by our company.
   A. are taken   B. were taken
   C. have been taken   D. will be taken

10. Sales have shown some improvement _____ we launched the new product last year.

    A. until   B. unless   C. since   D. although

Section B

Directions: *There are 5 incomplete statements here. You should fill in each blank with the proper form of the word given in brackets. Write the word or words in the corresponding space on the Answer Sheet.*

11. Be (care) _____ while crossing the roads and remember that they drive on the left in England.

12. The new suitcase at the exhibition (design) _____ by a Chinese company.

13. The related information can help you to operate the machine (efficient) _____.

14. The project is still under (discuss) _____, and practical solution are expected to be found.

15. According to the report, the North American health market (grow) _____ at a rate of about 7.4% in 2017.

Part II   Reading Comprehension

Directions: *This part is to test your reading abilities. There are 5 tasks for you to fulfill. You should read the materials carefully and do the tasks as you are instructed.*

Task 1

Directions: *Read the passage and make the correct choice.*

The 12th lunar month in Chinese is called *layue* (the month to worship all the deities). The eighth day of the 12th lunar month is the Laba Festival. It is treated as the beginning of the Chinese holiday season. After the Laba Festival, people enter into the busy preparation for the Lunar New Year. The main activity of the Laba Festival is cooking and sharing the special gruel (Laba-zhou).

Most people believe it has a close relation to Sakyamuni, the Buddha. He left his comfortable home and set off in search of the final enlightenment. After days of traveling without rest, he collapsed near a river in northern India. He was revived by a wandering shepherdess, who offered him her lunch of family leftovers consisting of sticky cereal, glutinous rice, dates, chestnuts and wild fruit. After consuming this repast, Sakyamuni took a bath and sat under a tree for meditation, where he finally attained enlightenment. The very day was the 8th day of the last lunar month.

1. At the Laba Festival, people _____.
   A. worship all the deities
   B. begin preparations for the Lunar New Year
   C. cook a variety of food to mark the occasion
   D. eat a special gruel together
2. The Laba Festival is believed by many to be related to _____.
   A. Confucianism   B. Buddhism
   C. Taoism   D. Christianity
3. Sakyamuni left his home and searched for _____.
   A. wealth for life   B. wisdom of life
   C. comforts of life   D. remedies for life
4. Sakyamuni ate a meal which was made of all the following except _____.
   A. wild fruit   B. rice   C. cereal   D. meat
5. The 8th of the last lunar month was remarkable because that day Sakyamuni _____.
   A. ate a meal given by a shepherdess
   B. found the meal very delicious
   C. made a deep meditation
   D. obtained the final enlightenment

Task 2

Directions: *Read the following diagram or picture and make the correct choice.*

6. Yogurt contains many nutrients except _____.
   A. calcium   B. protein   C. fat   D. probiotics
7. The bacteria in yogurt can _____.

    A. harm your stomach   B. add flavor to it
    C. do good to digestion   D. be creamy

8. You can drink orange soda _____.
    A. one cup a day   B. as much as you like
    C. once a day   D. twice a day

9. Too much soda drink can _____.
    A. have much more nutritional value
    B. take place of other nutritional value
    C. do good to your body
    D. ease digestive problems

10. Comparatively speaking if you want to be more healthy you should choose _____.
    A. yogurt   B. orange soda
    C. coffee   D. coca-cola

Task 3

Directions: *Read the following passage. After reading it, you should complete the information by filling in the blanks **in no more than three words** in the table below.*

    The NBMC Series is essential to your success in achieving permanent weight control. Diet Center believes when you become educated in nutrition (营养), you are then able to make wise, nutritional choices. You, and you alone, are responsible for yourself. Weekly classes are scheduled where you will be taught the principles of sound nutrition, self-direction, behavior modification (修改) and exercise. You will learn how your body functions, how stress affects the body and how to deal with that stress. You will also learn meal planning and food preparation techniques that will help you as well as your family. Positive changes in eating habits will be reinforced (加强) to ensure permanent weight control. The NBMC Series is offered at no additional charge.

If you want to achieve 11. _____ weight control you need to have 12. _____ 13. _____ choices can be made when you're educated in weekly classes, where you will learn the principles of sound nutrition, your body functions, the ways to deal with the stress that 14. _____ your body as well as learn meal planning and 15. _____ that will be quite useful to you.

Task 4

Directions: *The following is a list of terms. After reading it, you are required to find those items given in Chinese in the table below. Then you should put the corresponding letters in the brackets.*

A—Hairdresser
B—Art Director
C—Costume Designer
D—Sound Effect
E—Producer
F—Director
G—Starring
H—Best Boy

I—Stunt Coordinator
J—Title
K—Set Decorator
L—Editor
M—Visual Effect
N—Sound Mixer
O—Director of Photography
P—Production Manager

Example: （A）发型　　　　　　（J）字幕
16.（　）导演　　　　　　（　）制片主任
17.（　）主演　　　　　　（　）场务助理
18.（　）制片人　　　　　（　）布景
19.（　）声音合成　　　　（　）剪辑
20.（　）美术　　　　　　（　）摄影

Task 5

Directions: *Read the following passage. After reading it, you are required to complete the answers that follow the questions. You should write your answers **in no more than three words**.*

Letter One

March 16, 2001

Dear Mrs. Gently,

A friend of mine is giving a big party at her home to celebrate her wedding anniversary. My husband and I received an invitation that included this note at the bottom:

"In order to help pay for the food and drinks, you are asked to make a contribution of $10 at the door."

Don't you think this is incredibly (难以想象的) rude? I think we refuse the invitation, but my husband says we should go to the party and pay the $10. He tells me that Jim (my friend's husband) is out of job at the moment, so they are really short of money.

What do you think?

Puzzled in Peoria

Letter Two

March 25, 2001

Dear Puzzled,

In all my many years of giving advice on matters of taste and manners, I have never heard of such a ridiculous solution to financial embarrassment. Does your friend think that she's operating a restaurant? The lack of money does not excuse such rudeness. If your friend wants contributions from guests, she should plan an informal potluck dinner. It's perfectly acceptable to ask guests to bring a main dish or salad or dessert to a party. It is truly taste less to ask for a contribution of money.

My advice is simple. You should politely but firmly decline this "invitation."

Mrs. Gently

21. What are the two letters about?

    They are about matters of _____.

22. What is the purpose of the first letter?

    It is written for _____.

23. What is Mrs. Puzzled's husband's point of view?

    They should _____ and pay for the sum.

24. What is Mrs. Gently's advice?

    Declining the invitation _____.

25. What is a "potluck dinner?"

    It's _____ to ask a guest to bring a dish.

Part Ⅲ Translation (English into Chinese)

1. The library is trying in every possible way to raise more money to meet its increasing running costs.

    A. 这个图书馆正想尽一切办法提高收费标准并不断降低经营管理成本。

    B. 这个图书馆正尝试用各种办法提高收费标准以便尽早收回投资成本。

    C. 这个图书馆正想尽一切办法筹集更多资金满足越来越多的日常开支。

2. There is other information which will help you to know more about the training school.

    A. 这里还有资料供你参考，帮你了解学校培训情况。

    B. 你对学校培训已有所了解，没有必要再索取信息。

    C. 还有其他信息来帮助你更多地了解这所培训学校。

3. I believe my education background and experience in team work fit in nicely with the job requirements.

   A. 我认为这个团队应该招聘像我这样受过教育并有经验的人。
   B. 我相信我的学历和团队工作经历完全符合这一职务的要求。
   C. 我相信我受过的教育和经历完全能够适应团队工作的需要。

4. Candidates applying for this job are expected to be skilled at using a computer and good at spoken English.

   A. 申请该岗位的应聘者应熟练使用计算机并有良好的英语口语能力。
   B. 本项工作的申请人希望能提高使用计算机的能力并善于说英语。
   C. 本工作的受聘人员在应聘前应受过使用计算机的训练并懂得英语。

5. STUDENTS NEWSPAPER is looking for a journalist. Applicants should be studying at the university now, and should have at least one year's experience in writing news reports. The successful applicant will be expected to report on the happenings in the city and on campus. If you are interested, please send your application to the STUDENT NEWSPAPER office before the end of June. For more information, please visit our website.

   _____
   _____
   _____
   _____

Part Ⅳ Practical Writing

Directions: *This part is to test your ability to do practical writing. You are required to write a letter of application according to the information given below in Chinese. Remember to do your writing on the Translation/Composition Sheet.*

说明：假定你叫王林，根据下列内容写一封求职信。写信日期：2010 年 12 月 19 日

内容：

1）从 2010 年 12 月 10 日《中国日报》上获悉 BAC 公司招聘办公室秘书职位的信息；
2）毕业于东方学校（注：专业自拟），获得多种技能证书；
3）曾在 DDF 公司兼职，熟悉办公室工作，熟练使用电脑；
4）随信附上简历；
5）希望能获得面试机会。

注意信函格式

Words for reference:

中国日报 China Daily　工商管理　Business Administration　证书　certificate　附上　enclose

Supplementary Reading

Passage A

True Generosity　真正的慷慨

When a tornado touched down in a small town nearby, many families were left devastated. Afterward, all the local newspapers carried many human-interest stories featuring some of the families who suffered the hardest.

One Sunday, a particular picture especially touched me. A young woman stood in front of a totally demolished mobile home, an anguished expression twisting her features. A young boy, seven or eight years old, stood at her side, eyes downcast. Clutching at her skirt was a tiny girl who stared into the camera, eyes wide with confusion and fear. The article that accompanied the picture gave the clothing sizes of each family member. With growing interest, I noticed that their sizes closely matched ours. This would

一场龙卷风突袭我家附近的一座小镇，那里的许多家庭都损失惨重。随即，当地所有报纸都刊登了许多富有人情味的故事，重点报道一些受灾最为严重家庭的情况。

一个周日，一张特别的照片深深地打动了我的心。照片上，在一座完全被毁坏的活动房屋前，站着一位年轻妇女，痛苦的表情扭曲了她的面容。在她身旁，站着一个七八岁的小男孩，目光低垂。还有一个年龄更小的女孩，拽着年轻妇女的裙摆，睁大了眼睛紧盯着相机镜头，目光里充满了困惑与恐惧。在照片配发的报道中，给出了这个家庭每位成员的衣服尺寸。由于格外关注，我注意到他们衣服的尺寸与我家人的尺寸很接近。这将是一个教育孩子们的良机，可以让他们学会

be a good opportunity to teach my children to help those less fortunate than themselves.

I taped the picture of the young family to our refrigerator, explaining their plight to my seven-year-old twins, Brad and Brett, and to three-year-old Meghan. "We have so much, and these poor people now have nothing," I said. "We'll share what we have with them."

I brought three large boxes down from the attic and placed them on the living room floor. Meghan watched solemnly as the boys and I filled one of the boxes with canned goods and other nonperishable foods, soap and other assorted toiletries.

While I sorted through our clothes, I encouraged the boys to go through their toys and donate some of their less favorite things. Meghan watched quietly as the boys piled up discarded toys and games. "I'll help you find something for the little girl when I'm done with this," I said.

The boys placed the toys they had chosen to donate into one of the boxes while I filled the third box with clothes. Meghan walked up with Lucy, her worn, faded, frazzled, much-loved rag doll hugged tightly to her chest. She paused in front of the box that held the toys, pressed her round little face into Lucy's

帮助那些比自己还不幸的人。

我把那个年轻家庭的照片贴在冰箱上,并向我那7岁的双胞胎儿子——布拉德和布雷特以及3岁的小女儿梅根解释了他们的困境。"我们拥有这么多东西,而这些可怜的人此刻却一无所有,"我说,"我们应该与他们共同分享自己的东西。"

我从阁楼上拿下来三个大箱子,把它们放在客厅的地板上。梅根一脸认真地看着我和两个儿子一起把一些罐头和其他保质期较长的食品以及肥皂和其他洗漱用品装进其中一个大箱子。

我一边收拾衣服,一边鼓励儿子们去清理一下他们的玩具,然后把一些不太喜欢的捐献出来。男孩子们把不要的玩具堆成一堆,而梅根只是静静地看着。"等把这些物品整理完之后,我来帮你给那个小女孩挑选一些东西,"我对梅根说。

男孩子们把他们选好的准备捐献的玩具放进另一个箱子里,而我把第三个箱子装满衣服。这时,梅根走了过来,怀里紧紧抱着露西——一个她非常喜欢的布娃娃,虽然它很破旧而且已经褪色。她在装玩具的那个箱子前停下来,圆圆的小脸紧贴在露西扁平的彩妆娃娃脸上,最后亲吻了它一

flat, painted-on-face, gave her a final kiss, then laid her gently on top of the other toys. "Oh, Honey," I said. "You don't have to give Lucy. You love her so much."

Meghan nodded solemnly, eyes glistening with held-back tears. "Lucy makes me happy, Mommy. Maybe she'll make that other little girl happy, too."

Swallowing hard, I stared at Meghan for a long moment, wondering how I could teach the boys the lesson she had just taught me; for I suddenly realized that anyone can give their cast-offs away. True generosity is giving that which you cherish most. Honest benevolence is a three-year-old offering a treasured, albeit shabby doll to a little girl she doesn't know with the hope that it will bring this child as much pleasure as it brought her. I, who had wanted to teach, had been taught.

The boys had watched, open-mouthed, as their baby sister placed her favorite doll in the box. Without a word, Brad rose and went to his room. He came back carrying one of his favorite action figures. He hesitated briefly, clutching the toy, then looked over at Meghan and placed it in the box next to Lucy. A slow smile spread across Brett's face, then he jumped up, eyes twinkling as he ran to retrieve some of his prized Matchbox cars. Amazed, I realized that the boys

下。然后，将它轻柔地放在其他玩具的最上面。"噢，宝贝，"我说，"你不必把露西捐出来，你是那么喜欢它。"

梅根眼里闪着泪光，郑重地点了点头："妈妈，露西让我快乐，也许，她也会给那个小女孩带来快乐的"。

我一时噎住，久久地凝视着梅根，不知该如何把梅根刚才给我上的这一课转授给儿子们。因为我突然意识到，任何人都可以把他们弃之不用的东西捐献给别人，而真正的慷慨却是把你最珍爱的东西拱手相送。一个3岁的孩子把最珍爱的布娃娃——尽管它有些破旧——送给一个陌生的小女孩，希望能给她带去同样的快乐，这才是纯粹的仁爱。而我，本来想教育孩子们，结果却从梅根那儿受到了教育。

看着小妹妹把她最喜爱的娃娃放进箱子里，男孩们都惊讶地张大了嘴巴。布拉德一语不发，起身走进他的房间，拿出他最喜欢的人形公仔玩偶。他紧紧地抓着玩具，稍做犹豫，然后看了看梅根，把它放进箱子里，放在露西的旁边。布雷特的脸上慢慢绽出了笑容，他跳起来，眼睛闪闪发光，跑回房间拿来了几个他最珍爱的火柴盒汽车。我很吃惊地意识到，儿子们也领悟到了小梅根举动的意义。强忍着泪水，我把他们三个搂入怀中。

had also recognized what little Meghan's gesture meant. Swallowing back tears, I pulled all three of them into my arms.

Taking the cue from my little one, I removed my old tan jacket with the frayed cuffs from the box of clothes. I replaced it with the new hunter green jacket that I had found on sale last week. I hoped the young woman in the picture would love it as much as I did.

It's easy to give that which we don't want any more but harder to let go of something that we cherish, isn't it?

像小梅根一样,我把那件袖口已经磨破的茶褐色旧夹克从衣箱里取出来,换了一件我上星期刚买的墨绿色夹克,重新放进去。我希望照片上的那个年轻妇女也会像我一样喜欢它。

对我们来说,把不再需要的东西送与他人是很容易的。但是送出我们最珍爱的东西却难得多。难道不是这样吗?

Passage B

On Eagles' Wings 鹰翼之上的遐想

In the middle of a beautiful day I felt lost and the world came crashing in on me. I didn't know which way to turn except to head out to the country. On days like this I love to go where silence rules and the wind in the tall pine trees sounds like ocean waves along some deserted beach I've walked along in my memory.

I called home to tell Marianne I needed to think. She knows my "thinking days" and, as much as she most likely despises them, she says, "OK. I love you!"

At first I headed to the city park. Not

在晴好的一天中午,我感到迷惘,好像整个世界突如其来压在我的身上。我不知道该去往何处,只能向乡村进发。在这样的日子里,我喜欢去一静谧之所,在那里,风从高大松林间穿过,好像是拍打着记忆中我所走过的人迹罕至的海滩的波涛。

我给家里打电话告诉玛丽安我需要静思。她知道我所谓的"静思日",同样她很可能对此嗤之以鼻。但她还是说:"好吧。我爱你!"

起初我直奔城市公园。那虽不很有

very country but close enough to begin my journey inward. I told her I was going to where I used to take my kids...when I still had kids. That might give you an idea of what my down day was all about. My kids grew up, and I didn't.

After getting my fill of moms and dads running, laughing and swinging their time away together with their five year olds, I headed out to a nearby state park. Here ducks and cranes, rabbits and deer all steal your attention and replace the hurt of the day with awe and wonder. Here in the lateness of winter and the long wanting of spring, life stands still, as we humans know it. Here the birds fly where they want and when. The snow of colder days still holds on with its chilling grip. The ground is soft and muddy, giving hope to eagerly waiting grass that very soon will awaken from its dormant life and carpet once again the hills and pathways of the park's residents and visitors alike.

But I, sitting alone in my car, listen to songs that bring back memories of "Daddy days" and challenges of a daring feat to "Walk across the creek on this log like me, Dad!"

It is nearly spring and with it the winds cry out "I dare you!" and the child in us all heads to the attic to dust off the kite that takes us higher every year. On one end of the string are glorious colors like floating rainbows. On the other end

乡村的感觉，但是足够近可以开始我的内心之旅。我告诉她我要到过去常常带孩子们去的地方……当我仍然还和孩子们共同生活的时候。那也许会使你想到今天我为何而失落。我的孩子们已经长大，而我却没有做好心理准备。

脑子里塞满了父母们和他们五六岁的孩子们一起奔跑、嬉笑，共同消磨时光的情景，之后我又驱车前往附近的州立公园。在这里，鸭子、仙鹤、野兔和小鹿不由得吸引了我的注意力，油然而生的敬畏与惊奇取代了今日的伤痛。在这里，正值晚冬时节以及对春天的漫长期盼之中，正如我们人类所知，生命是落寞的。在这里，鸟儿们自由飞翔。寒冷冬日的残雪仍然借着严寒的余威覆盖大地。地面松软、泥泞，给那些焦急等待的小草以希望，很快他们将从沉睡中醒来，再次覆盖座座小山以及供园中居民和游客们行走的条条小径。

而我此时却独自一人坐在车里听着歌曲，回忆往昔——想起孩子们幼时称呼我"爹地"的好时光以及他们用大胆的壮举向我挑战"爸爸，像我这样从小溪上面的原木上走过来！"

春天就要来了，伴随着春的脚步，阵阵寒风哭嚎着"我怕你！"，未泯的童心促使我们都奔向阁楼掸掉那每年带着我们飞得更高的风筝上的灰尘。在线的一端是犹如飘动的彩虹般的缤纷的色彩。而另一端则是已长大的孩

grownup kids who swear that they "just want to get it started. You can take over in a minute, honey."

I, with all my troubles and woes, much too sensitive to life to begin with, discover that life goes on for everyone else even when yours stops for a while.

Then I met a man with bigger problems than I. He appeared to be in his seventies. Although careful with his steps, he seemed quite spry for his age. He stood near the edge of the road with a kite spindle in his hands. Seemingly lost for a moment, he stared skyward.

The string ended just beyond the tall tree and floated across two more, nestling the kite atop the highest branch of what seemed to be the tallest tree in the park. I walked over and without speaking a word, stood beside the man and gazed in amazement at what he had accomplished.

There, for all the world to see, was his grandson's kite. How perfectly it landed and how appropriate it was.

It was a replica of a beautiful Bald Eagle with wings spread wide open. As the wind rushed through the tree tops the plastic eagle's wings fluttered and flapped. It looked so real.

Alas, the only solution the man had was to cut the string. His grandson

子们，他们立下誓言"我们只是想让它启程飞翔。宝贝，你很快就会接过风筝线独自放飞它。"

带着烦恼与哀伤，并且对即将开始的生活过度敏感，我发现即使你自己的生活稍作停顿，对其他所有人来说，它仍然一如既往继续向前。

此后，我遇到了一个比我麻烦还要大的老先生。他看上去70岁左右。虽然他每走一步都很谨慎，但和他年龄比起来，他步履矫健。他站在路边，手里拿着一个风筝线轴。他凝望天空，似乎沉醉其中有一阵了。

风筝线正好在那棵高树的上方到头，飘荡着穿过另外两棵树，使风筝挂到了看上去似乎是公园里最高的那棵树的最顶端的枝条上。我走过去，一言不发地站在那位老先生的旁边，惊奇地注视着他的"杰作"。

正如所有人所见，那是他孙子的风筝。它降落得何其完美，位置多么恰当。

那是一只尽力伸展双翅的秃鹰风筝。当风从树间急速吹过，那只塑料鹰的翅膀便一张一合，振翅欲飞，看上去像真的一样。

唉，这位老先生唯一的解决办法便是切断风筝线。他的孙子相信爷爷

believed Grandpa could solve any problem. Perhaps even climb up and get it.

"You wanted it to fly as high as it could, Billy, didn't you?"

"Yes, Grandpa. But I wanted to keep it forever."

"There just comes a time when the only thing you can do is to cut the string and let it go. By doing that, perhaps when it takes flight like an eagle does, it will come back to us," the grandfather said.

I watched the old man cut and release the kite as Billy's dream with wings snapped back and gently settled into its new position high atop the barren tree.

As the two walked away, I looked to the sky and saw my answer too. Tears ran down my cheek and with a big sigh I prayed…

"Today I have to cut the final strings that kept my two boys within my reach. I have trained them to fly like eagles. But I wanted to keep them forever. Maybe by doing this, when they too take flight like the eagle does, they will come back to me someday."

The best lessons in life are learned by living it.

Keith, Evan: You are eagles. Now fly!

能解决任何难题。也许甚至还能爬到树上,把风筝摘下来。

"比利,你想让它飞得尽可能高,是吗?"

"是的,爷爷。但是我想永远拥有它。"

"眼下你唯一能做的只能是切断风筝线,让它去飞吧。那样做的话,或许当它像鹰一样展翅翱翔时,它会回到我们身边。"爷爷说。

我注视着这位老先生切断风筝线,松开了风筝。比利那带着翅膀的梦想旋即复飞,又轻轻地落在了位于那棵光秃秃的树顶端的新位置上。

看着祖孙二人渐渐走远,我仰望天空,看到了我的答案。眼泪顺着脸颊滚落。我长叹一声,心中不住地祈祷……

"今天我必须切断把我的两个儿子绑在我身边的丝线。我已经训练他们像鹰一样飞翔。但是我想永远拥有他们。也许切断了丝线,当他们也能像鹰一样自由翱翔之时,他们某一天也将会回到我身边。"

生活中的最好启迪是通过亲身经历而获得的。

基思,埃文:你们已经是雄鹰。现在,展翅腾飞吧!

Unit Four

Part I Vocabulary & Structure

Section A

Directions: *In this section, there are 10 incomplete sentences. You are required to complete each one by deciding on the most appropriate word or words from the 4 choices marked A, B, C and D. Then you should mark the corresponding letter on the Answer Sheet with a single line through the center.*

1. Some of the employees in the company are _____ to work at flexible hours.
   A. taken   B. achieved   C. allowed   D. formed

2. Please call us for more information as our website is currently_____ construction.
   A. under   B. by   C. of   D. with

3. _____, the sales manager began his report with the statistics of last month's sales.
   A. By now   B. As usual   C. So far   D. At most

4. We really appreciate our working environment, in _____ there was open, friendly workplace communication.
   A. how   B. what   C. whom   D. which

5. A company meeting provides an opportunity to _____ ideas and discuss any problems that come up within the workplace.
   A. reach   B. share   C. take   D. lead

6. Big changes have taken place at the Marketing Department _____ the new manger came.
   A. before   B. after   C. since   D. while

7. He said he would continue to support us _____ we didn't break the rules.
   A. as well as B. as soon as C. as far as   D. as long as

8. The school was _____ in 1929 by a Chinese scholar.
   A. established B. placed   C. imagined   D. made

9. We have reached an agreement _____ we should invest in the Internet-related business.

      A. what   B. where   C. that   D. as

10. _____ the excellent service, guests can enjoy delicious food in our restaurant.

      A. In place of   B. In addition to
      C. In charge of   D. In case of

Section B

Directions: *There are 5 incomplete statements here. You should fill in each blank with the proper form of the word given in brackets. Write the word or words in the corresponding space on the Answer Sheet.*

11. We are looking forward to (receive) _____ your early reply.

12. The main purpose of (educate) _____ is to teach students to think for themselves.

13. I was told that their project (complete) _____ last week as scheduled.

14. It is (general) _____ believed that about 14% of new cars can have electrical problems.

15. As a newcomer, almost everything in the company seems to be (interest) _____ to me.

Part II Reading Comprehension

Directions: *This part is to test your reading abilities. There are 5 tasks for you to fulfill. You should read the materials carefully and do the tasks as you are instructed.*

Task 1

Directions: *Read the passage and make the correct choice.*

    In ancient times wealth was measured and exchanged in things that could be touched: food, tools, and precious metals and stones. Then the barter system was replaced by coins, which still had real value since they were pieces of rare metal. Coins were followed by fiat money, paper notes that have value only because everyone agrees to accept them.

    Today electronic monetary systems are gradually being introduced that will transform money into even less tangible forms, reducing it to a series of "bits and bytes," or units of computerized information, going between machines at the speed of light. Already, electronic fund transfer allows money to be instantly sent and received by different banks, companies, and countries through computers and telecommunications devices.

1. Which of the following would be the most appropriate title for the passage?
   A. International Banking Policies
   B. The History of Monetary Exchange
   C. The Development of Paper Currencies
   D. Current Problems in the Economy

2. According to the passage, which of the following was the earliest kind of exchange of wealth?
   A. Bartered foods.
   B. Fiat money.
   C. Coin currency.
   D. Intangible forms.

3. The author mentions food, tools and precious metals and stones together because they are all _____.
   A. useful items
   B. articles of value
   C. difficult things to obtain
   D. material objects

4. According to the passage, coins once had real value as currency because they _____.
   A. represented a great improvement over barter
   B. permitted easy transportation of wealth
   C. were made of precious metals
   D. could become collector's items

5. Which of the following statements about computerized monetary systems is NOT supported by the passage?
   A. They promote international trade.
   B. They allow very rapid money transfers.
   C. They are still limited to small transactions (交易).
   D. They are dependent on good telecommunications systems.

Task 2

Directions: *Read the following ads and make the correct choice.*

2BR/2BA Apartment in Bloomingdale for only $1,320-1,340

COME IN TODAY! THESE PRICES INCLUDE HEAT, GAS, WATER & TRASH!

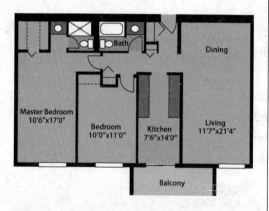

2 BEDROOM / 2 BATH
Sq Footage: 882 -924 sqft.
SECURITY DEPOSIT
Low $400 Security Deposit (if qualified)
PET POLICY
Cats OK, No Dogs
LAUNDRY
Shared-In Every Building
Wilshire Towers Apartments
201 Regency Drive
Bloomingdale, IL 60108
Tel 630-893-4400
wilshire@townmgmt.com
www.liveatwilshiretower.com

DESCRIPTION:

*Low $1,320 pricing INCLUDES HEAT, GAS, WATER & TRASH! Spectacular Savings!

*Newly renovated kitchens and baths

*Bright, eat-in kitchens with balcony access

*Open living rooms offer options for home office or formal dining

*Large walk-in closets

*Concrete construction provides quiet living

*Intercom access and elevators in each building

*Convenient business center with internet access

*Beautiful, park-like setting

*Two miles from I-355; I-290

*Near shopping, movie theaters, fine restaurants and exercise facilities

*Outstanding 24hr on-site service team

6. If you want to rent the apartment you should pay for _____.
 A. gas   B. water   C. heat   D. deposit

7. The surrounding environment of the apartment is convenient except for _____.
 A. shopping and movies   B. parks and lakes
 C. business and transportation   D. restaurants and exercise

8. If you want to share the apartment, your roommate will not allowed to

_____.
    A. keep pets   B. keep cats   C. keep dogs   D. hold parties
9. Your roommate and you can have separate _____.
    A. kitchen   B. bath   C. balcony   D. office
10. Laundry service is provided _____.
    A. 24 hours   B. in every apartment
    C. in the laundry center   D. by yourself

Task 3

Directions: *Read the following passage. After reading it, you should complete the information by filling in the blanks **in no more than three words** in the table below.*

Give a kid a hand!

    The first five years of a child's life are critical, the experts tell us. That's when their characters are formed. That's when caring is important. Someone to show them how to do things. Someone just to hold them. Unfortunately, for many of the world's children, that's just what they don't get. And society suffers as a result because a child without these has a lot less chance of growing up a well-developed adult. Some of us believe we can change things or at least try. And we need your help. No, don't reach for your pocket. It's not your money it's you we want. In your community there are dozens of ways you can make personal contact with kids and make a difference to their lives. Maybe you'll help one to read, to play a game, to learn to laugh. Maybe you'll just be the hand that holds out a little hope…

    Come on—help us give a kid a hand!

    Children develop their 11._____ in the first five years of their life and need people's 12._____ most.

    If children can't develop well, the whole 13._____ will be harmed.

    Your personal 14._____ with children is more important than your money.

    You can help these children by attending activities in your 15._____.

Task 4

Directions: *The following is a list of terms. After reading it, you are required to find those items given in Chinese in the table below. Then you should put the corresponding letters in the brackets.*

A—Space Flight   I—Express Train
B—Conducted Tour   J—Passenger Terminal
C—CA   K—Passenger Aircraft
D—Package Holiday   L—Director of Personnel
E—Package Tour   M—Travel Agency
F—Leisure Clothes   N—Traveler's Cheque
G—Urban Public Utilities O—Tourist Information
H—Single Room   P—Scenic Spots

Example: （ C ）中国民航   （ H ）单人房
16. （　）旅游信息   （　）宇宙飞行
17. （　）客运码头   （　）旅行社
18. （　）有导游的旅行   （　）快车
19. （　）城市公用设施   （　）休闲服
20. （　）景点   （　）团体旅游

Task 5

Directions: *Read the following passage. After reading it, you are required to complete the answers that follow the questions. You should write your answers **in no more than three words**.*

  Since its establishment, as a result of the high quality and the competitive prices of its products and the wide variety of designs available for selection by its customers, the X Group has been able to carry out effective marketing activities and build up a strong customer base. The Group currently has about 120 customers. Most of the artificial Christmas trees produced by the X Group are presently sold under the respective labels of its customers. Most of the X Group's products are sold directly or indirectly to retailers (零售商), importers in the U. S. , Canada, Europe, and trading companies or buying offices in Hong Kong.

  For the year ended 31ˢᵗ, January, 2002, the X Group's sales comprised approximately (大约) 68 percent to the U.S. , 20 percent to Europe, 7 percent to the Asia-Pacific region, and 2 percent to South America and other countries.

  21. What does the Group produce?
    It produces _____.
  22. What make its marketing a success?
    The _____ price and design of its products make its marketing a success.

23. How are its products sold?

They are sold under the labels of _____.

24. Which country or region is the second largest customer of the Group?

_____ is its second largest customer.

25. Compared with that in 1999, how much did Canada's imports from the Group in 2001 decrease?

Canada's imports decreased by _____.

Contents	1999	2000	2001
U.S.	62.70%	64.5%	67.8%
Europe	21.70%	23.3%	20.1%
Canada	9.40%	8.5%	7.2%
Asia-Pacific	4.5%	3.0%	3.2%
South America & others	1.7%	0.7%	1.7%

Part Ⅲ Translation (English into Chinese)

1. It would be natural to think all credit card issuers are honest; however, such is not always the case.

    A. 要特别注意信用卡使用者的诚信度，然而我们往往不会注意到这种情况。

    B. 诚信的人们会很自然地认为信用卡没有欺诈，但这种情况并非常常如此。

    C. 认为所有的信用卡发行商都很诚信是很自然的，然而情况并非都是如此。

2. You will tip about 10% in a British restaurant if the bill doesn't include a service charge.

    A. 英国餐馆通常收取服务费，有时另外还要你再付10%左右的小费。

    B. 在英国餐馆，如果餐费不包括服务费，你就要付10%左右的小费。

    C. 英国大约有10%的餐馆收小费，其余的餐馆还需要另外加服务费。

3. We have been doing business with you for many years and hope that you will make the best offer for us.

    A. 我们期待能够与你们建立起贸易关系，以合理的价格做生意。

    B. 我们同你们有多年的生意往来，希望能够给予我们最佳报价。

    C. 我们多年来一直与你们有生意往来，都是以最低价进行交易。

4. Whatever his or her job, the hotel person must possess or develop that quality called "service attitude."

    A. 无论谁到这家宾馆工作，每个人都应该不断提高文化素质并改善"服务态度"。

B. 在宾馆工作的任何人员，都应该首先具有较高的素质，从而养成良好的"服务态度"。

C. 宾馆工作人员无论做什么工作，都必须具备或养成称之为"服务态度良好"的素质。

5. Thank you for coming to the job interview at our office yesterday. With two weeks we will tell you our decision on your application. We want you to know that we will seriously consider your application. If, for some reason, we cannot offer you a position at this time, we will keep your application on the record. When there is a job opening, we will inform you immediately.

Part Ⅳ Practical Writing

Directions: *This part is to test your ability to do practical writing. You are required to write an invitation letter according to the information given below in Chinese. Remember to do your writing on the Translation/Composition Sheet.*

写信日期：2009 年 12 月 20 日

邀请人：UST 电子公司总经理 Mike Kennedy

被邀请人：张威

内容：UST 电子公司为庆祝公司创立三十周年，定于 2009 年 12 月 29 日（星期二）晚上 7 点在假日酒店举行庆祝晚宴。为了感谢张威先生多年来的支持和合作，UST 公司总经理邀请他出席庆祝晚宴。

Words for reference:

电子公司 Electronics Corporation   三十周年 30th anniversary   庆祝晚宴 dinner party   假日酒店 Holiday Inn

Supplementary Reading

Passage A

Finding Grace　寻找格蕾丝

"What could this possibly be?" I thought to myself. "Why would someone place that sign so low? No one could read it."

You see them everywhere. Small signs promoting yard sales, cars, and business opportunities are posted on poles and lobbies of stores throughout the community. So many, in fact, that they sometimes become a blur defeating the sole purpose of getting your attention.

Not this one. This one stood out because it appeared to be a mistake.

I had just arrived at the local shopping center and as I got out of my car I noticed a small sign taped to the first pole. The reason I noticed it was because it was taped to the very bottom of the pole.

At first I thought it had fallen, but at closer look I saw it had been very securely attached with several inches of masking tape. So much tape that it crossed over the middle of the sign

"那会是什么内容呢？"我暗自思忖，"为什么那张小广告被贴得这么低呢？没人会去看的。"

小广告随处可见。整个社区商店门口立柱和门厅贴满了小广告——清宅旧货促销的、卖车的，还有提供商业信息的。实际上，小广告贴得如此之多，有时成了模糊一片，完全失去了吸引人眼球的唯一目的。

这张广告则不是这样，这张广告之所以这么醒目，是因为它看上去像是贴错了地方。

我刚刚到达当地的购物中心，一钻出汽车，我就看到了粘在第一根柱子上的一张小广告。我注意到它，是因为它贴在柱子的最底部。

起初我以为它是从上端滑落下来的，但更仔细地瞧了瞧后，我发现它是用几英寸的遮蔽胶带牢牢黏着的。胶带太多了，从广告纸的中间缠过，遮住了上面的一些内容。

blocking out some of the details.

I had to look closer and to see what they were selling and who would do such a silly thing.

"Ah, a house for sale. I guess this was an approach to grab your attention," I said to a store clerk who was apparently taking a break and enjoying the fresh spring air.

"I don't think so," he replied.

"Well, why else would they have placed the sign way down here?" I asked.

Then, pointing down the walkway, he said, "That little girl is doing it. I just watched her and that lady hang this one."

Stooping down, I glanced to where he was pointing and indeed saw several more signs.

Curiosity always gets the best of me and some of the most incredible stories to share with my readers. This one was sure to fall into that category.

I slowly approached them and waited until the young child wound another yard of tape around the last sign.

"Excuse me. I don't mean to be

我不得不再靠近些细看，看看广告上要卖什么东西以及是谁会做这么愚蠢的事。

"啊哈，是卖房子的。我猜这是吸引人们注意的一种花招。"我对一位显然正在小憩并享受春日清新空气的店员说。

"我可不那么认为。"他回答道。

"是吗，那他们为什么要把这张广告贴这么低呢？"我问。

他沿着走道向下指了指，接着说道："那个小女孩还在贴呢。我刚刚看到是她和那位女士贴了这张。"

我俯下身，瞥了一眼他手指的方向，的确又看到了好几张广告。

好奇心总会让我甘拜下风，也总会让我获得一些最离奇的故事与我的读者分享。这件事当然属于这类故事。

我慢慢地靠近她们，耐心等待，直到那个小女孩又把一大段胶带缠绕在最后一张广告上。

"打扰一下，我并非有意无礼，只

rude, but why are you placing the house for sale signs so close to the ground?" I asked.

The woman smiled and turned to me. "She's not selling the house. Look closer," she said.

Again I stooped down adjusting my position until I could finally read the small print.

"We miss you!" I read out loud. I looked up and said, "I don't get it! You miss the house?"

"Look closer," the woman replied. "Look at the picture."

Okay, now I am really on my hands and knees. People passing by must have thought I was foolish.

"Do you see the child?" the woman asked.

"Yes, I do." I replied.

"Look to the left in front yard."

Now adjusting my glasses and squinting I said, "The dog? Do you mean the dog?"

"Yes! Look at the very bottom of the sign."

是想知道为什么你们要把售房广告贴得如此靠挨地面呢?"我问道。

那位女士边笑边转向我。她说:"她不是想卖房子。您再仔细看看。"

于是我再次弓下腰,并调整位置,直到我终于能看清广告上印的小字。

"我们想念你!"我大声读道。我抬起头说:"我真看不懂!你们想念房子吗?"

"再仔细看看。"那位女士答道,"看看那张照片。"

好吧,现在我可是真的跪撑在地上了。路过的人肯定会把我当成傻子。

"您看到那个小孩了吗?"那位女士问。

"是的,我看到了。"我回答。

"看前院的左侧。"

我正了正眼镜,眯着眼睛说,"狗?你是指那只狗吗?"

"对!看看广告的最下边。"

Now this was a test for sure.

"I miss you! Come home!"

I miss you come home? I didn't understand. Fighting to regain my dignity, I stood up. I must have had that confused look on my face.

"Her dog is lost," the woman explained.

"Most people would hang a lost sign with a picture of the dog on it. It would also be where people could actually see it," I said with a chuckle.

"Well, you saw it," the young girl said.

Good point.

I found myself distracted for a moment. This child had the most beautiful cherub-like face accented by short curly blonde hair that danced with every movement she made.

Just seeing her sky blue eyes twinkle with the innocence of her youthful spirit made me hesitate to ask for further explanation.

Thankfully, the woman filled me in. "I explained to her that it may be hard to find her dog. As you can see the store has many signs posted. So she said that she had a better idea. She wanted her dog to find her. Thus the picture of the house, her and the dog," she said.

这可真是个对我的考验。

"我想你！回家吧！"

我想你，回家？我不明白。我努力恢复自己的端庄形象，甚至站了起来。我的脸上肯定写满了困惑。

"她的狗丢了。"那位女士解释道。

"大多数人都会张贴一张附有狗照的寻狗启事，还应该把它贴在人们能真正看到的地方。"我咯咯地笑着说。

"是啊，你不就看到了。"那个小女孩说。

说得好。

我不由得怔了片刻。这个小女孩长着极其漂亮的娃娃脸，一头卷曲的金色短发随着她的动作跳来跳去。

看着她天蓝色的眼睛扑闪出年少活泼的天真无邪，使我迟疑着要不要再继续深问下去。

幸亏那位女士为我做了进一步的解释。

她说："我向她解释，也许很难找到她的狗了。正像你能看到的，这家商店贴了很多小广告。于是她说她有个更妙的主意。她说让狗找到她。所以，广告上的那张照片就是我们的房

"And hanging them down there..."
"You got it. So the dog could see it," she said.

Then motioning me aside the woman whispered, "It's been missing a few days now. We really thought it would be back already. I didn't want to give up until she felt she did everything she could."

My heart ached for the child as I tried to think of some way to help.

"What a great idea!" I said to her. Then I stooped down and said, "I will say a prayer. I'm going to give your mom my phone number. Call me when you and your dog are back together."

I handed the woman one of my business cards. I had to know how this ended. "By the way, what's your dog's name in case I meet him in my travels?" I asked.

"It's a girl dog," the child said. "Her name is Grace."

I looked to the woman and she confirmed.

"Yes, we named her that because that's how we got her. She was lost. 'Amazing Grace, I once was lost but now I'm found,'" the woman said

子以及她和狗。"

"并把广告贴在那么低的地方……"
"您终于明白了。这样狗就能看到这张广告了。"她说。

随后，那位女士示意我走到一旁，小声告诉我，"狗已经走失好几天了。我们真希望它已经回来了。在她觉得自己尽了全力之前，我不想放弃。"

我为这个孩子感到心痛，试图想个什么办法帮帮她。

"真是一个好主意！"我对她说。然后我俯下身子说，"我会为你祈祷的。我把我的电话号码留给你的妈妈。当你和你的狗重聚时，给我打电话。"

我把一张名片递给了她妈妈，我一定要知道这件事的结果。"顺便问一下，你的狗叫什么名字？也许我在旅途中会遇到它。"

"她是一只小母狗。"小女孩说，"她叫格蕾丝。"

我又看了看那位女士，得到了她的确认。

"是的。我们给她起这个名字是因为我们就是这么得到她的。她当时迷了路。'奇异恩典，我曾迷失，今被寻回。'"那位女士笑着说。

smiling. One week later my phone rang. The little girl called to tell me Grace came home. Amazing!	一周后，我的电话铃响了。那个小女孩打电话告诉我格蕾丝回家了。 太神奇了！

Passage B

Eight Gifts That Don't Cost a Cent　无须分文的八种礼物

This simple checklist can help measure how you are nurturing your relationships. **The Gift of Listening** But you must really listen. Don't interrupt, don't daydream, don't plan your response. Just listen. **The Gift of Affection** Be generous with appropriate hugs, kisses, pats on the back and handholds. Let these small actions demonstrate the love you have for family and friends. **The Gift of Laughter** Clip cartoons. Share articles and funny stories. Your gift will say, "I love to laugh with you." **The Gift of Solitude** There are times when we want nothing better than to be left alone. Be sensitive to those times and give the gift of solitude to others.	以下八种简单的"礼物"能帮助你培养人际关系。 学会倾听 但是你必须真正倾听。不要打断他人，不要心不在焉，不要思考应答。只是倾听。 表达情感 慷慨而恰当地拥抱、亲吻、轻拍后背以及握手。让这些微小的动作来表明你对家人及朋友的爱。 开怀大笑 剪下卡通漫画。与他人分享幽默的文章和有趣的故事。这些礼物表明"我愿与你一起开怀大笑。" 安静 有时我们只想安静。对这种情况应该善解，让他人独享安静。

The Gift of a Favor Everyday, go out of your way to do something kind.	施以恩惠 每天都行善积德。
The Gift of a Written Note It can be a simple "Thanks for the help" note or a full sonnet. A brief, handwritten note may be remembered for a lifetime.	短信 可以只是一张写着"感谢您的帮助"的纸片或是一首完整的十四行诗。简短的手写便条可能会使人终生难忘。
The Gift of a Compliment A simple and sincere, "You look great in red," "You did a super job," or "That was a wonderful meal" can make someone's day.	不吝赞扬 一句简单而真诚的赞扬,"你穿红衣服真漂亮。""你干得真棒。"或"这顿饭真可口。"之类的话会使人高兴不已。
The Gift of a Cheerful Disposition The easiest way to feel good is to extend a kind word to someone.	愉快性情 使人愉悦最简单的方法便是亲切的话。

Unit Five

Part I Vocabulary & Structure

Section A

Directions: *In this section, there are 10 incomplete sentences. You are required to complete each one by deciding on the most appropriate word or words from the 4 choices marked A, B, C and D. Then you should mark the corresponding letter on the Answer Sheet with a single line through the center.*

1. The task will not be fulfilled _____ we get help from other departments.
   A. if   B. unless   C. since   D. when
2. Vitamin B enables the body to _____ full use of the food taken in.
   A. make   B. reach   C. put   D. bring
3. These construction workers are required to participate _____ the safety training program.
   A. at   B. with   C. in   D. to
4. We'll send the memo in advance _____ all people can have enough time to get prepared.
   A. in case   B. so that   C. as if   D. ever since
5. Congratulations on the great _____ you've made since last year.
   A. progress   B. measure   C. appointment D. sense
6. I am very happy to declare that this year's sales target _____ ahead of time.
   A. achieved   B. has achieved
   C. has been achieved   D. had been achieved
7. The new traffic rules will become _____ from the first day of 2016.
   A. comfortable B. excellent   C. challenging D. effective
8. The news quickly spread throughout the campus _____ he won the first prize in the competition.
   A. which   B. what   C. that   D. who
9. The delivery of the goods was _____ because of the snow storm.
   A. worked out B. put off   C. turned on   D. taken in
10. When_____, the project will help to greatly improve the environment in

the community.

    A. finished   B. to finish   C. finishing   D. finish

Section B

Directions: *There are 5 incomplete statements here. You should fill in each blank with the proper form of the word given in brackets. Write the word or words in the corresponding space on the Answer Sheet.*

11. It is hard (guess) _____ what comments the manager will make on the design.

12. Payment can (make) _____ online from your checking or savings account.

13. This type of loan is (frequent) _____ used for this purpose.

14. It is possible that we reach a long-term (agree) _____ with the company.

15. I must admit that the situation is (difficult) _____ than I thought it would be.

Part II   Reading Comprehension

Directions: *This part is to test your reading abilities. There are 5 tasks for you to fulfill. You should read the materials carefully and do the tasks as you are instructed.*

Task 1

Directions: *Read the passage and make the correct choice.*

People often do strange things in the name of science. Recently, a group of volunteers at the University of Michigan were asked to take an unusual pills every day. The pill contained garlic (大蒜). Why garlic? Because researchers want to know if garlic reduces cholesterol (胆固醇) in the body. Cholesterol, a chemical that builds up on artery (血管) walls, is thought to result in heart disease. Evidence suggests that heart disease occurs less often in countries where people eat lots of garlic.

When these researchers fed rats a high cholesterol diet that included 2 percent garlic, the rats' cholesterol rose about 4 percent. Other rats on the same diet without garlic showed a 23 percent increase in cholesterol. Garlic must have kept the cholesterol levels down.

Now humans are being tested. Volunteers have their blood checked. They take garlic pills every day for a month. Then their blood is rechecked to see if the garlic has had any effect on their cholesterol level.

It's too early to tell; but scientists may someday have us eating garlic to stay healthy.

1. It is believed that cholesterol _____.
   A. helps lower levels in the blood
   B. causes brain damage only in humans
   C. brings about heart disease only in rats
   D. leads to heart diseases
2. The volunteers were asked to take garlic pills because _____.
   A. they were brave enough
   B. they helped do the scientific research
   C. they could be well-paid
   D. they liked eating garlic
3. Evidence shows that there are less heart diseases _____.
   A. in rats than in people
   B. in people than in rats
   C. in countries where people eat a lot of garlic
   D. in countries where people eat no garlic
4. Which of the following is TRUE according to the passage?
   A. The garlic pills look like garlic.
   B. The garlic pills are made of garlic.
   C. The main content of the garlic pills is garlic.
   D. The garlic pills contain a lot of cholesterol.
5. The result of the cholesterol study involving humans was _____.
   A. that garlic kept cholesterol levels down
   B. that iron kept cholesterol levels down
   C. that garlic had no effect on cholesterol level
   D. not mentioned

Task 2

Directions: *Read the following ads and make the correct choice.*

SAVE 20%
It's only a phone call away
MAYCOTT HOTELS

Over 30 five-star hotels all over the nation to suit your every need.

Reserve a room today, and you will save 20% on all rooms at Maycott "Room for the Day" (excluding tax) by using your American Express Corporate Card.

Due to seasonal demands, the availability of rooms may be subject to each hotel's situation. An advanced reservation, to be made by calling our toll free number 1-800-755-0090 at least 10 working days before your stay, is required to qualify for the discount.

6. Which of the following is NOT a condition placed on receiving the discount?
   A. A guest must use a specific type of credit card to pay for a room.
   B. The booking must be done well in advance of checking into the hotel.
   C. The reservation must be carried out by calling the toll free number.
   D. Guests must make their payments in cash.
7. What will the discount apply to?
   A. Accommodations.   B. Meals.
   C. Transportation.   D. Sales tax.
8. What can be implied from the advertisement?
   A. Most travelers don't make a habit of making reservations prior to checking in.
   B. There is a business relationship between the credit card company and the hotel.
   C. The hotel gets very busy during the summer season.
   D. It usually takes a minimum of 10 days for a credit card to clear.
9. How many hotels apply to the ads?
   A. At least 5.   B. At least 30.   C. At least 20.   D. At least 10.
10. The availability of rooms is variable according to _____.
   A. customers' needs   B. seasonal demands
   C. reservations   D. qualifications

Task 3

Directions: *Read the following passage. After reading it, you should complete the information by filling in the blanks **in no more than three words** in the table below.*

PURCHASE ORDER
                              No. BD/135
Messrs: China National Cereals, Oils & Foodstuff Import & Export Corp, Shengyang Branch, 23 Beihai Road, Shengyang

We confirm our agreement on purchase of the following goods:
Description: A-I Grade Canned Beef of the following four specifications:
   A. 225 GM net weight
   B. 350 GM net weight
   C. 425 GM net weight
   D. 450 GM net weight
Quantity: (Case)
   A. 500
   B. 400

        C. 400

        D. 600

Unit Price: CIF net New York per case in U. S. Dollars

        A. 36.20

        B. 40.50

        C. 50.60

        D. 38.40

Packing: By standard export case of 120 cans each

Payment: 100% by irrevocable(不能取消的) letter of credit opened immediately through First National City Bank, N.Y., and drawn at sight

Delivery: For Item A and B: Prompt shipment

Shipping Marks: On each and every case, the shipping mark should be printed

Remark: In addition to the ordinary shipping documents, please also submit Certificate of Origin for each shipment

---

Information About Purchase Order

11. The number of cans in each case: _____

12. CIF unit price of 425 GM net weight: _____

13. Letter of Credit opened through _____

14. Prompt shipment is needed for _____

15. On each case printed with _____

Task 4

Directions: *The following is a list of terms. After reading it, you are required to find those items given in Chinese in the table below. Then you should put the corresponding letters in the brackets.*

      A—Economic Growth   I—Business Operation

      B—Market Research   J—Profit and Loss

      C—Competitive Advantage   K—Health Insurance

      D—Cash Flow   L—Working Capital Budget

      E—Real Profit   M—Gross Profit

      F—Payroll Tax   N—Net Profit

      G—Financial Data   O—Application For Insurance

      H—The Profitability of the Enterprise

Example: (O) 申请保险　　　　　(F) 工薪税
16. (　) 业务经营　　　　　(　) 毛利
17. (　) 市场研究　　　　　(　) 利润和亏损
18. (　) 健康保险　　　　　(　) 竞争优势
19. (　) 现金流转　　　　　(　) 企业盈利率
20. (　) 实际利润　　　　　(　) 流动资金预算

Task 5

Directions: *Read the following passage. After reading it, you are required to complete the answers that follow the questions. You should write your answers **in no more than three words.***

Letter One

February, 2001

Dear Sirs,

It'll be the Valentine's in a couple of weeks. I'd like to have a bottle of red wine, plus a white rose, sent to my husband in Koln, Germany. His address there is, Herr Karl Ziegdreud, 105 Wilheimstrass, Koln, Germany, zip code 05524. I'd also like you to suggest a red wine, only that it should be strong-flavored, and a produce of the country. My customer's number is IDS-123-543ZQ#.

I hope both gifts should arrive at 9 o'clock, 14th February, local time.

Yours sincerely,

Yang Lihua

Letter Two

February, 2001

Dear Madam,

We have learnt about your needs through your mail. In the form below we have filled in your needs and your special requirements as you had mentioned. If there's anything inexact or you may wish to add, make changes as you please. If it's all clear, tick (给……打钩) them all and send it back to us. We shall do the rest for you.

Besides, we offer a 10-minute free international call for every customer between January 15 and February 25. Simply dial 800-, plus your customer number, and plus the number of the person you want to call, let it be your friend, relative or children.

We at Interflora all wish you a happy day with a great envy.

Yours truthfully,

Interflora

CONFIRM	ITEM	NUMBER	DESCRIPTION	PRICE PER UNIT(US$)	SUB-TOTAL
( )	Rose	1	White	15	
( )	Wine	1	Red, strong, local, 750 mL per case. Price to be determined.	15 to 48	

* All products taxed before delivery.

* Notification by telephone upon realization of payment through the Bank of China.

21. What is the company's name and its major business?

　　The company is specialized in _____ goods.

22. What are the woman's orders?

　　She orders a bottle of _____.

23. What is the company's response?

　　The company is ready for service and also offers _____ free international call.

24. How is the woman going to pay?

　　She is to pay through the _____.

25. If all items in the form are good, what is Yang Lihua supposed to do?

　　Tick them all and _____.

Part Ⅲ　Translation (English into Chinese)

1. All in all, the Smith's Company offered me the experience to advance my career in China.

　　A. 总而言之，史密斯公司的历程有助于我实现在中国发展事业的目标。

　　B. 总而言之，史密斯公司的历程使我认识到我应该在中国发展事业。

　　C. 总而言之，史密斯公司使我有了在中国拓展我的职业生涯的经历。

2. Candidates should be given the company brochure to read while they are waiting for their interviews.

　　A. 求职者应该帮助公司散发有关的阅读手册，同时等候面试。

　　B. 在阅读了公司所发给的手册之后，求职者才能等待面试。

　　C. 在求职者等待面试时，应该发给他们一本公司手册阅读。

3. Candidates applying for this job are expected to be skilled at using a computer and good at spoken English.

　　A. 申请该岗位的应聘者应熟练使用计算机并有良好的英语口语能力。

　　B. 本项工作的申请人希望能提高使用计算机的能力并善于说英语。

　　C. 本工作的受聘人员在应聘前应受过使用计算机的训练并懂得英语。

4. First of all, I appreciate your advice on my decision to go to work in the

computer company.

A. 我首先感谢你的建议，我已决定去一家电脑公司工作了。

B. 首先，很高兴到贵公司来听取你们在计算机方面的意见。

C. 首先，感谢你对我决定去那家电脑公司工作所给予的建议。

5. WORKTRAIN is a website for jobs and learning. It puts the most popular services for job seekers online. This makes it easy for you to get the information you need. At this site, you'll find over 300,000 jobs, plus thousands of training opportunities and information on job market. And because WORKTRAIN uses the power of the internet, it gives you what you need faster and more easily than ever before.

Part Ⅳ Practical Writing

Directions: *This part is to test your ability to do practical writing. You are required to write a notice according to the information given below in Chinese. Remember to write the notice on the Translation/Composition Sheet.*

说明：写一份英语通知，涵盖以下内容，不要逐词翻译。东方电子有限公司为一家中外合资企业，主要生产制造电子产品，该公司将于2007年12月26日（星期三）在我校学生俱乐部举行招聘会，招聘的职位有：办公室秘书、市场营销人员和实验室技术员。我们希望有兴趣的学生于当天下午1:30到2号会议室参加招聘会，并请携带身份证、个人简历、英语应用能力考试合格证书以及计算机等级证书。

Words for reference:

招聘 recruit   身份证 ID card   实验室技术员 laboratory technician   B级证书 the certificate of PET (level B)

Notice

Dong Fang electronics Ltd. is a joint venture, which _____

Supplementary Reading

Passage A

What Are You Made for   天生我材必有用

My older sister filled out thirteen college applications. She sent them all around the country—to Seattle, Chicago, Philadelphia, Houston. Then she sat back and waited for the replies, for the big fat envelopes, confident in her perfect GPA and her valedictorian's cap.

Three years later, my own applications sat before me. They were all terrifyingly blank. I didn't know what to say.

"What do you do in a typical day?" one question asked. How could I answer? The truth was that I stayed home all day. After my mom dropped me off at school I would pretend to go inside, then sneak back out across the soccer fields, catch the subway, and either go home or to the bookstore across the street. There I'd stay until my parents came home. When they asked if I wanted to go out, I'd tell them I'd had a busy day and was too tired. Forget extracurricular. All I did was sleep, and when I couldn't sleep, read.

"What do you see in your future?" asked another question. But I didn't see

我的姐姐填写了 13 份大学申请表。她把它们寄往全国各地——西雅图、芝加哥、费城、休斯敦。然后,她便安心静候回音,等待那些又大又厚的信封,因为她对自己的完美的平时成绩以及优秀毕业生的身份感到颇为自信。

三年以后,我自己的申请表也放在了面前。那是令人恐慌的空白。我不知道该写些什么。

"你在某个有代表性的日子里通常做些什么?"其中一个问题这样问我。事实是我整天待在家里。我妈妈开车把我送到学校以后,我便假装走进校园,然后穿过足球场偷偷溜出来。搭乘地铁,或者回家,或者到街对面的书店。我在那儿一直待到父母回家。如果他们问我是否想出去,我就会告诉他们,我度过了忙碌的一天,实在太累了。忘掉一切课外活动,我所做的全部事情就是睡觉。有时无法入睡,我便看书。

"你对自己的未来有什么预计?"另一个问题被问道。但我什么也没有。

anything. "You should apply to as many schools as you can," said my dad. "Keep your options open."

He couldn't know that all of my options were closed. There was no way any college would accept me, no matter how smart I was, with weeks of school skipped and failing grades. Of course, I couldn't tell my dad that. I'd been lying to him—and everyone else—for months. I hid my report cards in a dark corner of my closet and deleted the concerned messages from my teachers off the phone.

So I took all of the applications and carefully put each one, mostly still blank, into an envelope. Sealed them, addressed them, and showed them to my father. Thirteen applications, just like his other perfect daughter. We mailed them together.

One day, about a month later, I snuck home early from school, only to find my parents sitting on the couch with sad, serious looks on their faces. "We're worried about you," they said. "We know there's something wrong. The school called and said you haven't been there since last week."

I started to cry. "I'm sorry," I said. "I can't do it anymore. I used to like school—I still like learning—but I just can't do it anymore."

"你应当尽量申请更多的学校。"爸爸说，"暂时不要做最后的决定。"

他没法知道我已毫无选择了。无论我有多聪明，由于我数周的逃课记录和不及格的成绩，任何一所大学都不可能接纳我。当然，我不能把这些告诉我的爸爸。数月来，我一直对他以及其他所有人撒谎。我把成绩单藏进壁橱黑暗的角落里，并把来自老师们的相关信息从电话中删除。

然后，我拿起申请表，小心翼翼地把每一份表格放进信封里封好，尽管绝大部分仍是空白的。写好地址把它们拿给爸爸看。十三份申请信，就像他另外那个优秀的女儿一样。随后我们一起去把信邮走了。

一个月后的一天，我早早从学校溜回家，却发现我的父母坐在沙发上，脸上满是伤感而严肃的表情。"我们为你担心。"他们说。"我们知道一定是出什么问题了。学校打来电话说，你从上周起就没有上学。"

我开始大哭起来。"对不起。"我说，"我再也不能那样做了。我过去喜欢上学，现在我仍然喜欢学习，但是我只是不想再那样做了。"

"Do what?"

"Get up in the morning. I can't stand being up before the sun rises; I feel like a ghost. I fall asleep in all my classes. Not that it matters—not that they teach me anything I want to know. They won't let me write stories or talk about politics or anything else I might actually want to do. How do you expect me to get up every morning for that?"

My parents brought me to a psychiatrist, who said I was depressed. I could have told him that. But when he said it, suddenly no one was angry anymore. My teachers all told me they would help me catch up with my work. The principal told me I wouldn't be disciplined for skipping weeks of school.

So I went back to school, and it was just about bearable. At least I didn't feel so guilty about lying to everyone all the time.

But I couldn't stop thinking about those blank applications. Did it matter if I finished high school, if I wasn't even going to college? What was the point?

I was just about to give up again when I got a phone call.

"Hello, this is Susan. I'm calling from the admissions office at Hampshire College."

"做什么？"

"早晨起床。我无法忍受在日出前起床。我感觉自己就像一个幽灵。所有课上我都昏昏欲睡。还不只是这些，课上老师不讲我所想学的东西。他们不让我写小说，不让我谈论政治或者不让我做其他我可能确实想要做的事情。你们怎么能期望我为那些事情而早起呢？"

父母带我去看精神病医生。他说我患了抑郁症。我本来可以告诉他那些事情。但当他说出这个字眼，一瞬间没有人再对我表示气愤了。我所有的老师都告诉我，他们会帮我补上功课。校长也告诉我，我不会因逃课而受到处分。

于是我又返回了学校，对此我几乎可以忍受了。至少，我不会因为过去总是对大家说谎而感到过分愧疚。

但是，我仍然一直想着那些空白的申请表。如果我高中毕业，如果我没能上大学，那些申请还很重要吗？有什么意义呢？

就在我将要再次放弃的时候，我接到了一个电话。

"您好，我是苏珊。我在汉普郡学院招生办给你打电话。"

Hampshire College? I remembered the name. It was the only college I had even bothered trying to fill out the form for.

"We were wondering about your application," she continued. "Your SAT scores are very high, as are your grades until this year. But it looks like last semester you failed three classes, and the application itself was only half filled out. What's going on?"

"I've been depressed," I said, and then, before I could stop myself: "I couldn't stand school anymore. I couldn't take one more test. I'm not a robot, I'm not made like that."

I expected her to hang up on me. But instead she just asked, "What are you made for?"

So I told her about the stories and the poems that I wrote, how I loved politics and had twice interned with a local congressman, how I liked to read books about psychology and evolution and the beginning of the universe. I told her that I was made to learn, not to take tests or be told what to think. I told her that I was getting treatment for depression, but if college was anything like high school, I didn't want to go.

"Some colleges may be like that," she said, "but not Hampshire. We

汉普郡学院？我记得这个名字。这是唯一一所我耐着性子努力为之填写申请表格的院校。

"我们想了解你的申请情况。"她继续说道，"你的 SAT 考试成绩非常高。之前你的成绩也很优秀。不过看起来，上学期你有三门功课不及格，而且申请表也只填了一半。发生了什么事吗？"

"我一直都很抑郁。"我说，然后我难以控制地继续说道，"我再也无法忍受学校了。我再也不能参加考试了。我不是机器人，我生来不是为了做那些事的。"

我以为她会挂断电话，但是相反她只是问道，"你生来是为了做什么？"

于是，我告诉她，我写的小说和诗歌，我如何爱上了政治，并曾经两次随当地议员实习，以及我如何喜欢阅读关于心理学、进化论和宇宙起源方面的书籍。我告诉她，我生来是为了学习，不是为了参加考试，或者被告诉要思考什么问题。我告诉她，我正在接受抑郁症治疗，但是如果大学和高中完全一样，我就不想去了。

"一些大学或许是那个样子。"她说，"但是汉普郡学院不是那样。我们

believe that every student should get to choose what they want to learn, to define their own education. It takes a special kind of student to succeed at Hampshire, and we think you're one of them."

"You do?" I asked.

"This is unofficial," she replied, "but I just wanted you to know that in a few weeks you're going to get a letter offering you admission to Hampshire."

It wasn't likely my depression disappeared with those words. But to suddenly have a future again—to be told that a college wanted me in spite of my failing high school—maybe even because I couldn't succeed at a regular high school or college—because I was different, independent, special... that was enough to get me to finally fight against my depression, to love and believe in myself and, years later, to be happy.

相信每个学生都能选择他们想要学习的内容，来界定自己的教育。在汉普郡学院获得成功需要一种特殊的学生，我们认为你就是其中的一员。"

"真的吗？"我问道。

"这是非正式的意见。"她回答道，"但是我只是想让你知道，几周后，你将收到汉普郡学院的录取通知书。"

我的抑郁症不可能随着她的那些话语而消失。但是，突然间，我再次拥有了未来——得知一所大学不顾我高中成绩不及格却要录取我——也许甚至是因为我不可能在常规的高中或大学里获得成功——因为我与众不同、独立而特别……这些足够使我最终战胜我的抑郁症，让我去爱并相信自己，从而数年后，使自己变得快乐。

Passage B

Taking a Stand　坚定你的立场

The summer before fifth grade, my world was turned upside down when my family moved from the country town where I was born and raised to a town near the beach. When school began, I found it difficult to be accepted by the kids in my class who seemed a little more sophisticated, and who had been in

上五年级之前的那个暑假里，我家从生我养我的乡下小镇搬到了一座海滨小城，从此我的生活发生了翻天覆地的变化。等到开学的时候，我发觉自己很难被班里的其他同学所接纳。他们看起来有些过于世故。而且他们从一年级起就同在一个班级。

the same class together since first grade.

I also found this Catholic school different from the public school I had attended. At my old school, it was acceptable to express yourself to the teacher. Here, it was considered outrageous to even suggest a change be made in the way things were done.

My mom taught me that if I wanted something in life, I had to speak up or figure out a way to make it happen. No one was going to do it for me. It was up to me to control my destiny.

I quickly learned that my classmates were totally intimidated by the strict Irish nuns who ran the school. My schoolmates were so afraid of the nuns' wrath that they rarely spoke up for themselves or suggested a change.

Not only were the nuns intimidating, they also had some strange habits. The previous year, my classmates had been taught by a nun named Sister Rose. This year, she came to our class to teach music several times a week.

One day during music, I announced to Sister Rose that the key of the song we were learning was too high for our voices. Every kid in the class turned toward me with wide eyes and looks of total disbelief. I had spoken my opinion to a teacher—one of the Irish nuns!

与此同时，我还发现天主教会学校有别于我以前就读的公立学校。在原来的学校里，学生可以直言不讳地向老师表达自己的想法。而在这里，哪怕是建议按照事情原本的规律做一下改变也被认为是忍无可忍的粗鲁行为。

妈妈曾经教导我：如果在生活中我想得到某种东西，就必须大胆直言或者千方百计找出办法使梦想成真。没有人能代替我做这一切。只有我才能掌控自己的命运。

很快我便了解到全班同学都早已被管理这所学校的那些严厉的爱尔兰修女们镇住了。全校学生都对这些修女的坏脾气怕得要死。以至于几乎没人为自己辩解或提议做出某种改变。

这些修女不仅常常吓唬学生而且她们自身还有一些怪异的习惯。去年，一个被叫做罗丝姐姐的修女一直都担任我那些同学的老师。而在今年，她每周只是来我所在的班级上几次音乐课而已。

有一天在音乐课上，我大声告诉罗丝老师，对我们的嗓音来说，正在学唱的这首歌调门实在太高。班里的每个孩子都转过头，瞪大了眼睛盯着我，脸上满是难以置信的表情。我竟敢对老师——一名爱尔兰修女，说出了自己心中的想法。

That was the day I gained acceptance with the class. Whenever they wanted something changed, they'd beg me to stick up for them. I was willing to take the punishment for the possibility of making a situation better and of course to avoid any special attention from Rose. But I also knew that I was being used by my classmates who just couldn't find their voices and stick up for themselves.

Things pretty much continued like this through sixth and seventh grades. Although we changed teachers, we stayed in the same class together and I remained the voice of the class.

At last, eighth grade rolled around and one early fall morning our new teacher, Mrs. Haggard—not a nun, but strict nevertheless—announced that we would be holding elections for class representatives. I was elected Vice President.

That same day, while responding to a fire drill, the new president and I were excitedly discussing our victory when, suddenly, Mrs. Haggard appeared before us with her hands on her hips. The words that came out of her mouth left me surprised and confused. "You're impeached!" she shouted at the two of us. My first reaction was to burst out laughing because I had no idea what the word "impeached" meant. When she explained that we were out of office for

正是在那一天，全班同学真正接纳了我。从此，每每他们想让某些事情有所改变，他们就来恳求我为他们仗义执言。为了使大家的处境变得好些，我心甘情愿接受惩罚。同时，还要避免引起罗丝老师的过多关注。但是我也心知肚明，全班同学是在利用我，因为他们从未大胆直言，为自己的利益而据理力争。

诸多此类事情持续不断发生，历经六年级和七年级。尽管我们更换了不同的老师，但是我们仍然在同一个班级，我始终是大家的代言人。

终于，我们开始了八年级的学习生活。一个初秋的早晨，我们的新老师哈嘉德夫人——虽然她不是修女，但仍然很严厉——宣布我们准备选举班级干部。于是我被推选为副班长。

就在同一天，我们参加了消防训练。正当我和新班长激动不已地讨论我们的胜利的时候，突然，哈嘉德老师两手叉腰出现在我俩面前。她脱口而出的话令我既惊愕又困惑。"你们被弹劾了。"她对我俩吼叫着。我的第一反应是开怀大笑起来因为我根本不知道她所谓的"弹劾"是什么意思。当她向我们解释我俩因为在消防训练中闲聊而被撤职时，我蔫了。

talking during a fire drill, I was devastated.

Our class held elections again at the beginning of the second semester. This time, I was elected president, which I took as a personal victory. I was more determined than ever to represent the rights of my oppressed classmates.

My big opportunity came in late spring. One day, the kids from the other eighth grade class were arriving at school in "free dress," wearing their coolest new outfits, while our class arrived in our usual uniforms: the girls in their pleated wool skirts and the boys in their salt and pepper pants. "How in the world did this happen?" we all wanted to know. One of the eighth graders from the other class explained that their teacher got permission from our principal, Sister Anna, as a special treat for her students.

We were so upset that we made a pact to go in and let our teacher know that we felt totally ripped off. We agreed that when she inevitably gave us what had become known to us as her famous line, "If you don't like it, you can leave," we'd finally do it. We'd walk out together.

Once in the classroom, I raised my hand and stood up to speak to our teacher. About eight others rose to show

第二学期伊始，我们班再次选举。这次，我被推选为班长。我把这看作是个人的胜利。我比以往更加坚定，决心代表受压迫的全班同学的利益。

在晚春时节，我的机会来了。一天，我发现八年级某个班级的学生身着便装来上学。他们穿着最酷的新套装。而我们却照例一如既往地穿着校服，女生一律穿着羊毛料百褶裙，男生一律穿着黑白相间的格子裤。怎么会有这种事情呢？我们都想探个究竟。来自那个班级的一名学生告诉我们他们的老师获得安娜校长的许可，可以给他们这种特殊待遇。

我们十分气愤，大家约好一起去找老师，想告诉她我们完全被愚弄了。我们全都同意如果她仍不可避免地说出那句早被我们熟知的"名言"——"如果你不喜欢，你就可以走。"那么我们就会真的那样做。一起走出教室。

最终在教室里，我举手示意并站起来对老师说出了我们的想法。有七八个同学也同时站起来表示支持。我

their support. I explained how betrayed we felt as the seniors of the school to find the other eighth graders in free dress while we had to spend the day in our dorky uniforms. We wanted to know why she hadn't spoken on our behalf and made sure that we weren't left out of this privilege.

As expected, instead of showing sympathy for our humiliation, she fed us her famous line, "If you don't like it, you can leave." One by one, each of my classmates shrank slowly back into their seats. Within seconds, I was the only one left standing.

I began walking out of the classroom, and Mrs. Haggard commanded that I continue on to the principal's office. Sister Anna, surprised to see me in her office so soon after school had begun, asked me to explain why I was there. I told her that as class president, I had an obligation to my classmates to represent them. I was given the option to leave if I didn't like the way things were, so I did. I believed that it would have been a lie for me to sit back down at that point.

She walked me back to class and asked Mrs. Haggard to tell her version of the situation. Mrs. Haggard's side seemed to be different from what the class had witnessed. Then something incredible happened. Some of my classmates began shouting protests from

解释道：我们看到其他八年级学生可以身着便装而我们却不得不穿着老式的校服度过一整天。作为本校高年级学生，我们有一种被出卖的感觉。我们想知道，老师为什么没有为我们仗义执言，从而确保我们也能拥有这一特权。

果然不出所料，她没有对我们受到的不公平待遇表现出一丝同情，而是甩出那句著名的老话："如果你不喜欢，你就可以走。"于是所有同学一个接一个慢慢地缩回到座位上。很快，只剩下我一个人还站在那里。

我迈步走出教室。哈嘉德老师命令我一直走，去找安娜校长。刚刚开始上课，就看到我来到校长办公室，安娜校长感到很惊讶，她问我为什么来找她。我告诉她作为班长，我有责任代表全班同学表达心声。我被赋予权利，如果我不喜欢目前事情运作的方式，我可以选择离开。在那种情况下，我相信如果我重新回到座位坐下，对我来说，那完全是一种撒谎。

安娜校长陪我一起走回教室。她让哈嘉德老师讲述一下她对这件事情的说法。然而哈嘉德老师的说法与先前同学们看到的情况大相径庭。随即，令人难以置信的事情发生了。一些同学在他们的座位上大声抗议来回应哈嘉德老师的言论。"那不是真的。"他

their desks in response to Mrs. Haggard's comments. "That's not true," they countered. "She never said that," they protested.

It was too much of a stretch for them to stand up and walk out with me that day, but I knew something had clicked inside of them. At least they finally spoke up.

Perhaps they felt that they owed me. Or they realized that we'd soon be at different high schools and I wouldn't be there to stick up for them anymore. I'd rather believe that when they spoke up that day, they had finally chosen to take control of their own destinies.

I can still hear their voices.

们反驳道,"她根本不是那么说的。"

我深知,那天随我一起站起来并走出教室对其他同学来说实在是强人所难了。但是他们的内心还是受到了某种触动。至少他们最终大胆地说出了自己的想法。

也许他们感觉亏欠了我。或者他们意识到我们不久就要升入不同的中学,而我将不能在那里继续为他们仗义执言了。我更愿意相信那一天当他们大声说出心里话的时候,他们终于选择由自己掌控自己的命运。

时至今日,我依然可以听到他们的喊声。

Unit Six

Part I Vocabulary & Structure

Section A

Directions: *In this section, there are 10 incomplete sentences. You are required to complete each one by deciding on the most appropriate word or words from the 4 choices marked A, B, C and D. Then you should mark the corresponding letter on the Answer Sheet with a single line through the center.*

1. Please _____ us of your decision and we will act according to it.
    A. give   B. inform   C. take   D. make

2. The company makes it possible _____ the market information with its partners.
    A. share   B. sharing   C. to share   D. shared

3. It has been unusually cold this winter and experts say it's not _____.
    A. normal   B. different   C. necessary   D. important

4. _____ our great surprise, our company has made much more profit than we expected last year.
    A. For   B. In   C. With   D. To

5. I did not _____ to meet you here far away in this country.
    A. think   B. see   C. expect   D. guess

6. I wish I could have attended the job fair yesterday, but I _____ it.
    A. missed   B. would miss   C. miss   D. will miss

7. We are so busy this week that we have to _____ the meeting till next week.
    A. give away   B. put off   C. take over   D. set out

8. It is with great pleasure _____ I accept your offer to join the club.
    A. which   B. whom   C. who   D. that

9. To fully enjoy your trip, we hope you will make a detailed plan _____.
    A. on purpose   B. in reality   C. by accident   D. in advance

10. Do you think such a small company will be capable of_____ this large order?
    A. handling   B. handled   C. to handle   D. handle

Section B

Directions: *There are 5 incomplete statements here. You should fill in each blank with the proper form of the word given in brackets. Write the word or words in the corresponding space on the Answer Sheet.*

11. When there is something (serious) _____ wrong, people usually expect an apology.

12. The workers in the factory demanded that their pay should (raise) _____ by 20 percent.

13. My (person) _____ view is that the price they offer is quite competitive.

14. It seems that this method is (effective) _____ than the previous one.

15. Researchers found several important (different) _____ in the way boys and girls learn a foreign language.

Part II   Reading Comprehension

Task 1

Directions: *Read the following passage and make the correct choice.*

If you have an AT&T Business Direct account, you can have your telephone bill paid automatically each month. You can make payments online with a bank account or use one of the following credit cards: *visa, master card, Discover Network or American Express*. When you make an online payment, please follow the instructions given below.

Instructions

1. To make your payment online, click the "Pay Now" link under the "Account Overview" summary.

2. If your business has more than one registered account, first select the account you need from the "Account Number" menu, and then click the "Pay Now" link.

3. If you have never made an online payment before, you will be asked whether you want to make a payment by using a bank account or credit card. Select either "Bank Account" or "Credit Card" from the "Select payment Method" menu.

The online payment system is available Monday through Saturday, from 7:00 a.m. to 12:00 a.m.(Midnight) Eastern Time.

1. An AT&T Business Direct account helps you _____.
    A. earn an interest from a bank account
    B. make the first month's payment only

  C. pay your telephone bill automatically
  D. enjoy all the available banking services
 2. The payment with an AT&T Business Direct account can be made online with _____.
  A. a passport   B. a credit card
  C. a driving license   D. a traveller's check
 3. If you have several registered accounts for payment, the first link that you should click is _____.
  A. the "Select Payment Method" menu   B. the "Account Overview" summary
  C. the "Account Number" menu   D. the "Pay Now" link
 4. When making the first-time online payment, you will be asked to _____.
  A. register your online account number B. open several registered accounts
  C. select the payment method first   D. apply for a new credit card
 5. The passage is mainly about _____.
  A. how to pay phone bills by AT&T Business direct
  B. how to open an AT&T Business Direct account
  C. how to make use of online bank services
  D. how to start a small online business

Task 2

Directions: *Read the following passage and make the correct choice.*

 If you own a car, you are probably considering buying some kind of car insurance. However, when you are actually purchasing car insurance, it can be difficult for you to decide which is your best choice. The ideal buying process is to first research and decide, then purchase.

 Research first

 Before buying car insurance, you should find out the purpose of your purchase and how the insurance meets your needs.

 Decide on suitable Car Insurance Policies

 A neglected part of car insurance is the part which covers medical bills. Medical payments can add up very quickly in an accident situation, and the insurance should cover the bills incurred both by you and by the passengers in your car. Make sure you know the full value that your insurance covers.

 Purchase the best Car Insurance for your needs

 You have a number of choices when it comes to the actual purchase of the car insurance. Each has advantages and disadvantages, and these may be influenced by your individual taste and previous buying experience. Insurance companies may offer you good advice, but prices on the Internet are often better.

6. According to the first paragraph, when buying car insurance, one should first _____.

    A. decide on the number of policies to purchase
    B. do careful research on different choices
    C. choose the best insurance company
    D. look for the lowest insurance rate

7. The purpose of research is to find out whether the car insurance _____.

    A. includes all the advantages   B. best meets your needs
    C. offers the best rate   D. is easy to purchase

8. When buying car insurance, people often neglect _____.

    A. the damage to the car
    B. the bills paid by the passengers
    C. the part covering medical bills
    D. the background of the insurance company

9. According to the last paragraph, your choice of car insurance may also be influenced by _____.

    A. your driving habits
    B. the kind of car to be insured
    C. the attitude of your family members
    D. your own taste and buying experience

10. Which of the following might be the best title of the passage?

    A. Medical Bills Covered in Car Insurance
    B. Importance of Buying Car Insurance
    C. Advice on Buying Car Insurance
    D. Advantages of Car Insurance

Task 3

Directions: *Read the following passage. After reading it, you should complete the information by filling in the blanks marked 11 to 15 (**in no more than 3 words**) in the table below. You should write your answers on the Answer Sheet correspondingly.*

Ladies and gentlemen,

    Good afternoon. We hope that visit here will be a pleasant one. Today I would like to draw your attention to a few of our laws.

    The first one is about drinking. Now, you may not buy wine in this country if you are under 18 years of age.

    Secondly, noise. Enjoy yourselves by all means, but please don't make unnecessary noise, particularly at night. We ask you to respect other people who may wish to be quiet.

Thirdly, crossing the road. Be careful. The traffic moves on the left side of the road in this country.

My next point is about rubbish. It isn't lawful to drop rubbish in the street. When you have something to throw away, please put it in your pocket and take it home, or put it in a dustbin.

Finally, as regards smoking, it is against the law to buy cigarettes or tobacco if you are under 16 years of age.

I'd like to finish by saying that if you require any sort of help or assistance, you should contact the local police, who will be pleased to help you.

Now, are there any questions?

A Few Pieces of Advice

The laws to follow: law on ___11___, noise, traffic, rubbish and smoking

Allowing and forbidding: not allowed to buy wine but can buy cigarettes or tobacco if he is between ___12___ years old

Keep quiet: do not make a noise especially ___13___

Traffic: moves on the ___14___ of the road

Rubbish-throwing: put the rubbish in your ___15___ and take it home or throw it into a rubbish box

---

Task 4

Directions: *The following is a list of words used in public signs (公共标语). After reading it, you are required to find the items equivalent to (与……等同) those given in Chinese in the table below. Then you should mark the corresponding letters in order of the numbered blanks, 16 through 20, on the Answer Sheet.*

A—Take Care Not to Leave Things Behind
B—Ladies' Room
C—Hands Off
D—Staff Only
E—Beverage Not Included
F—Please Keep off the Grass
G—Beware of Pickpockets
H—No Photos
I—For Use Only in Case of Fire
J—Shooting prohibited
K—Do Not Litter
L—Wet Paint
M—Lost and Found
N—Hold Handrail
O—Road Ahead Closed
P—Office Hours
Q—Dogs Not Allowed

Examples: （ K ）不要乱扔垃圾　　　　　（ N ）抓紧扶手
16.（　）闲人免进　　　　　　　（　）灭火专用
17.（　）女洗手间　　　　　　　（　）酒水另付
18.（　）油漆未干　　　　　　　（　）失物招领处
19.（　）前方道路封闭　　　　　（　）小心扒手
20.（　）办公时间　　　　　　　（　）禁止狩猎

Task 5

Directions: *Read the following passage. After reading it, you are required to complete the answers that follow the questions (No.21 to No.25). You should write your answers* ***in no more than 3 words***.

December 1

Dear Mr. Dias,

　　Further to your letter of 22 November, I am very happy to say that we are now in a position to confirm our participation in the *Sao Paulo Trade Fair* (圣保罗商品交易会).

　　We would be very grateful if you could send us a plan of the exhibition hall and indicate which areas are still available and the respective prices.

　　We would like to participate for all four days of the fair and estimate that we would need a display area of approximately 100-120 square meters. I will be able to confirm this information once I have received your plan and price schedule.

　　I would also be very grateful for any information on the expected visitor number and on your marketing campaign. This information would be invaluable in fixing our budget for the exhibition.

　　We are quite keen to move quickly on this and secure the best display area available. Therefore, I would very much appreciate a quick reply from you.

　　I look forward to hearing from you soon.

　　Yours sincerely,

Oscar Cornell,
Marketing Manager

21. What does Mr. Cornell want to confirm in the letter?

He wants to confirm _____ in the Sao Paulo Trade Fair.

22. What is Mr. Dias expected to send?

Mr. Dias is expected to send a plan of _____.

23. How long will the Sao Paulo Trade Fair last?

It will last _____.

24. What is invaluable for Mr. Cornell to fix their budget for the exhibition?

The information on the expected visitor number and on _____.

25. Why does Mr. Cornell require a quick reply from Mr. Dias?

Because he wants to get the best _____ available.

Part Ⅲ   Translation (English into Chinese)

1. Partly because of the increasing demand the prices of sea food in this region have almost doubled recently.

 A. 人们越来越认识到海产品的价值，因此都涌到这个地区争先抢购海鲜。

 B. 由于海产品很受人喜爱，消费量翻番，使得这个地区海鲜的价格猛涨。

 C. 这个地区海产品的价格近来几乎翻了一番，部分原因是需求日益增加。

2. Nowadays it is a well-known fact that second hand smoking does even more harm to human health.

 A. 二手烟对人类健康危害十分巨大，这在今天已经是无可争辩的事实。

 B. 二手烟对人类健康的危害甚至更大，这在今天已是众所周知的事实。

 C. 今天广为传播的说法已被证实，二手烟对人类的危害并非有意夸大。

3. Many good movies have been produced recently, but I still prefer to watch old movies because they are more interesting.

 A. 人们对电影是有兴趣的，特别是对老片子，所以我主张放映老片子。

 B. 近来拍了很多好的影片，既古老又饶有趣味，我觉得人人都喜欢看。

 C. 近来制作了很多好影片，但是我还是喜欢老片，因为老片更有趣。

4. This matter is so important that it should not be left in the hands of an inexperienced lawyer.

 A. 如此重要的事情，没有经验的律师不敢接手。

 B. 这件事事关重大，不能交给缺乏经验的律师来处理。

 C. 这件事也很重要，不应让没有经验的律师处理。

5. If you want to get a driver's license, you will have to apply at a driver's license office. There you will be required to take a written test for driving in that area. You will also need to pass an eye test, if you need glasses, make sure you wear them. In addition, you must pass an actual driving test. If you fail the written or driving tests, you can take them again on another date.

Part IV   Practical Writing

Directions: *This part is to test your ability to do practical writing. You are required to write an invitation letter according to the information given below in Chinese. Remember to do your writing on the Translation/Composition Sheet.*

发信日期：2011 年 3 月 15 日

内容：Sharon 和 Tracy 是大学同学，毕业后两年未见。现 Sharon 得知 Tracy 要到南京出差，特邀一聚，Sharon 将同 Tracy 游览玄武湖、中山陵等。请 Tracy 回信告知是否能有时间。

Words for reference: 玄武湖 Xuanwu Lake 中山陵 Dr. Sun Yat-sen's Mausoleum

Supplementary Reading

Passage A

Why Can't I Touch the Sky?　为何我不能触摸天空呢？

My six-year-old daughter Sophie and I were playing a rhyming game the other day and out of the blue she asked me, "Why can't I touch the sky?" I laughed inside and thought for a few moments. I tried to explain it from the Jack and the Beanstalk story, but she just	几天前，我和六岁的小女儿索菲一起在玩押韵游戏，她突然问我说："为何我不能触摸天空呢？"我心里暗笑，想了一会儿，便试着用"杰克和豆茎"的故事来给她解释。但她只是不解地看着我，一脸茫然。随后我又试着为她讲解老套的地球空间理论，

looked at me funny. Then I tried the old earth space thing, but that was too technical. The more I tried, the clumsier it got when finally I realized I wasn't getting through.

Then I had a realization. What if my daughter had asked the same question to another six year old? What would the other child have said? Some six year olds think they know the answer to everything and it's fun to listen to what they have to say. Something tells me her friend wouldn't have the slightest difficulty in explaining the answer. Chances are, they would have argued and discussed it until finally reaching agreement. I wished I could have turned the question over to an imaginary friend and then sit back and listen to the conversation.

That night while lying in bed, I kept thinking about her question and why I couldn't come up with a really cool answer. Was it because I had "grown up" and now used my imagination like an "adult"? As I grew, the maturation process obviously had boxed me in. And worse yet... I knew that someday, my little girl just might lose her pure and trusting imagination to adulthood and maybe stop asking these wonderfully creative questions.

I didn't feel like it was right that I progressed up the ladder of maturity only to lose what I feel is a very important

但这些说法过于专业了点。我越是解释，越是令她一头雾水。最终我意识到，我根本没法说清这个问题。

由此我有所感悟。如果我女儿向另一个六岁的孩子提出同样的问题，结果会怎样呢？那个孩子会说些什么呢？一些六岁的孩子认为，他们知道所有事情的答案，倾听他们童真的言语真是很开心的事。我觉得，她的小朋友会毫不费力就能给出这个问题的答案。当然，他们也很有可能会为这个问题而争论不休，直到最终达成一致的看法。我多么希望能把这个问题交给一位充满想象力的朋友来回答，然后悠然地坐在一旁倾听他们的谈话。

那天晚上我躺在床上，头脑里一直在想她提出的问题。我为什么不能给出一个很棒的答案呢？难道是因为我已经"长大"，而只能运用那种"成人"的想象力的缘故吗？随着我年岁的增长，显而易见，这一成熟的过程逐渐把我禁锢了起来。而更糟糕的是……我深知，终有一天我的小女儿也会长大成人，失去她天真烂漫的想象力，或许不会再问这种极富创造力的问题。

我并不认为这样的现象是好事，即在我一步步走向成熟的过程中，却失去了我认为是一种极为重要的观

concept: the ability to retain and possess a childlike quality to explore other possibilities. Where did my childlike imagination go? Why did it go? I thought I would ask Sophie this question to help me understand why some adults tend to lose sight of this magical way of thinking and why others make a living by it.

She looked at me with a puzzle on her face and then I knew. It never occurs to her that there's any other way. Why on earth would a six-year-old little girl dream she couldn't touch the sky unless somebody told her she couldn't?

I watch my little girl as she plays. She dresses her babies and gets them ready for their day. She conducts an imaginary reading class and makes sure each doll pronounces the words correctly. Her imagination takes wing each and every day to places I'm not aware. Sometimes I can catch a glimpse of her inner world when we sit and talk about her day or what her plans are for tomorrow.

Remember when we were younger, when we used to talk about and imagine what we would become when we grew up? I wanted to be a policeman and my friends wanted to be firemen and race car drivers. We believed anything was possible and we could become whatever we wanted, never doubting the possibilities. As children, we dreamed big.

念，即具有并保持探索其他可能性的童真性格。我那年幼时孩童般的想象力哪里去了？它为什么会失去？我想我会问索菲这个问题，以帮助我弄明白，为什么一些成年人往往会对这种不可思议的神奇思维方式视而不见，而另一些人却可以以此谋生。

索菲满脸困惑地看着我，顿时我豁然开朗。对她来说，根本就不存在其他的思维方式。究竟为什么一位六岁的女童会梦想她无法触摸天空呢？除非有人告诉她：她不能。

我注视着我的小女儿，她正在自娱自乐。她给每个娃娃穿好衣服，为他们开始新一天的生活做好准备。她给布娃娃们上想象中的阅读课，并确保他们都能发音准确。每一天，她的想象力都自由翱翔，飞向我无法知晓的地方。有时，当我们坐下来，谈论她当天的生活以及第二天的计划时，我才会窥见她的内心世界。

你还记得吗，在我们年少时，我们常常会谈论或想象长大后做什么的理想。我想过当一名警察，而我的朋友们却想成为消防队员和赛车手。我们相信一切都是可能的，我们会成为任何自己梦想担当的角色，而且从来没有怀疑过这样的可能性。作为孩子，我们都有远大梦想。

Children are visionaries, and it seems a little sad to think our childlike imagination seems to disappear as we grow older. As we age, the ever-increasing intrusions of the world on our minds seem to frighten that childlike imagination into full-blown retreat.

As we grew up, we learned why the sky really is blue, and why grass is green. Why flowers need sunlight and how birds really fly. We lose a little bit of the wonder of life around us as we schedule the next meeting or plan tomorrow's agenda.

I have my daughter to thank for asking her question. She made me think about my own potentiality and how I may be limiting myself. Maybe I need to reconnect with my childlike imagination and think more outside the box of adult creativity. If I do that, maybe I can explain in my own six-year-old way, why she can... touch the sky.

孩子们都是梦想家。然而想来令人略觉伤感的是，当我们逐渐长大，孩童般的想象力好像就随之消失了。随着我们年岁的增长，脑海中不断增长的对世界的了解似乎却迫使那孩童般的想象力全面消退。

随着我们的成长，我们懂得了为什么天空真的是蓝的，而草却是绿的。为什么花儿需要阳光以及鸟儿怎样真正飞翔。当我们总是按部就班地安排下一个会议或是筹划第二天的工作日程时，我们便对周围的生活失去了些许的新奇之感。

我要感谢我的女儿向我提出了这个问题。她促使我考虑自己拥有的潜能以及我可能怎样束缚了自己。或许我需要重拾昔日孩童般的想象力，从而摆脱成人创造力的桎梏来思考问题。如果我做到这一点，那么或许我就能用自己六岁时的思维方式来解释为什么她能……触摸天空。

Passage B

The Transformative Power of Gratitude 感恩的力量

My life was humming along last year when the universe delivered back-to-back wake-up calls. First, I lost my job when the magazine I edited went belly-up. A month later, my father landed in the intensive care unit. It felt as though life

去年我的生活原本过得一帆风顺，舒适安逸，但突然间上天打来一连串的唤醒电话，让我猛然醒悟，意识到一些不应被淡忘的东西。起初，我供职的杂志社倒闭，因此我也失业了。一个月后，我的父亲因

were peeling my layers, like a tree being stripped of bark.

Not knowing what else to do, I drove down to my parents' house. Their vulnerability terrified me. I visited my father at the hospital every day, trying to hold back tears as I stood awkwardly by his bed and stroked his thick white hair. At home, I cooked, answered the phone, and washed the dishes. One afternoon, I held my mother's hand as she wept. Its warmth and softness, its *aliveness*, astonished me. And that's when the most unexpected thought welled up from some fresh chink in my heart: *I am so blessed to be here right now.*

Suddenly, I felt lucky to have the time to be with my parents, to witness them, which I wouldn't have been able to do if I hadn't lost my job. Now, I had all the time there was.

I felt even more grateful for this gift of time when my father returned home. Grateful for the smallest things: poring over seed catalogues together, watching sitcoms with him, listening to his breathing while he slept in his recliner. Grateful for the cold wind on my face as I cross the supermarket parking lot on an errand for my parents. Grateful for my brother's love and care, for my mother's humanity, for the moon climbing the maple trees outside my old bedroom window.

病住进了重症监护病房。那种感觉就好像生活正在一层一层地啃噬我的肉体，就像树木被剥去外皮一样。

不知该如何是好，我只好驱车回到父母家中。他们的脆弱着实把我吓了一跳。每天我都去医院看望父亲。每当我局促不安地站在父亲的病床边，轻抚着他浓密的白发，我都强忍着不让泪水滚落。回到家里，我做饭，接电话，洗碗。一天下午，母亲抽泣起来，我紧紧握住她的手。母亲的手温暖、柔软，充满活力，令我惊诧不已。恰在此时，一种出乎意料的想法从我心底的裂隙中涌了出来：此刻我能待在这里是多么的幸福。

猛然间，我感到非常幸运能有时间与父母共处，时刻关注他们。而如果我没有失业的话，就绝不会做到这一点。如今我拥有了所有属于自己的时间。

尤其当父亲出院重返家中，我更加感谢这份时间的礼物。感谢那些与父亲共处的细微琐事：一起研读种子目录，和他一起观看情景喜剧，倾听他在躺椅上熟睡时的鼻息声。感谢当我跑腿为父母购物而穿过超市停车场时拂面而来的冷风。感谢我兄弟的关爱照顾以及母亲的慈爱，感谢月亮爬上我儿时那间卧室窗外的几棵枫树梢头。

Looking back, I never would have chosen the crises of my father's illness and losing work I loved. But my parents' vulnerability—and my own—frighten me less these days. Gratitude opened the gates of tenderness—right in the midst of fear and uncertainty.	回头想来，我绝对不愿选择父亲重病与自己失业的双重危机。但这些天来，父母以及自己的脆弱并未把我吓倒。恰好处在恐惧与迷惘之间，感恩为我打开了柔情之门。
Since then, I've started making a conscious effort to practice gratitude in some small way every day. When I do, I feel much more connected with the flow of life, instead of isolated and alone in my own struggles and fears.	从那以后，我开始每天有意识地在一些细微之处表达感恩之情。当我这样做的时候，我感觉与鲜活的生活联系得更加密切，而不是与世隔绝，独自生活在抗争与恐惧之中。
For me, gratitude can be a powerfully transformative practice, just as some psychologists have found that practicing gratitude can actually improve our emotional and physical well-being.	对我来说，感恩能够成为一个强大的自我改造的实践过程。正像一些心理学家已经发现的那样，感恩实际上能够提升我们情感与身体上的康乐感觉。

Unit Seven

Part I Vocabulary & Structure

Section A

Directions: *In this section, there are 10 incomplete sentences. You are required to complete each one by deciding on the most appropriate word or words from the 4 choices marked A, B, C and D. Then you should mark the corresponding letter on the Answer Sheet with a single line through the center.*

1. You can ask these experts _____ advice in job hunting.
   A. on   B. over   C. from   D. for
2. If you want to get there before dark, you should start your journey _____.
   A. at times   B. at once   C. in person   D. in detail
3. The play was so boring _____ I could hardly keep myself from falling asleep.
   A. that   B. which   C. what   D. whether
4. We hope that our customers can _____ advantage of this new service.
   A. have   B. carry   C. take   D. bring
5. The unemployment rate has become much lower _____ the government took these measures.
   A. but   B. since   C. if   D. while
6. The rope is not strong enough to _____ the weight of the big case.
   A. conduct   B. produce   C. make   D. support
7. He attended school in England for several years, after _____ he returned home.
   A. what   B. that   C. which   D. whom
8. You can trust our product as we have _____ control over its quality.
   A. strict   B. limited   C. little   D. natural
9. A new study finds out that a kid can learn without _____ what he is doing.
   A. realize   B. realized   C. realizing   D. to realize
10. _____ last year, traffic accidents have decreased by 10% this year.
    A. Related to   B. Compared with   C. Concerned about   D. Dealt with

Section B

Directions: *There are 5 incomplete statements here. You should fill in each blank with the proper form of the word given in brackets. Write the word or words in the corresponding space on the Answer Sheet.*

11. You'd better make a phone call (check) _____ whether the e-mail has been received.

12. We had been working for almost 16 hours, and we (final) _____ finished the task.

13. The Prize in Economics (establish) _____ in 1968, that is, more than half a century ago.

14. He is thinking of (leave) _____ his job and going to Germany for further study.

15. Most people attending his lecture have found that they have learned something (use) _____.

Part II   Reading Comprehension

Task 1

Directions: *Read the following passage and make the correct choice.*

When you speak on the telephone, you cannot use your facial expression, eye contact and gestures to help communicate your message. You voice must do the job.

A good voice is pleasant to listen to because it communicates a positive message. Keep in mind the following qualities of a good voice:

Speak in a voice neither too loud nor too soft. Speak louder when giving important information.

Speak slowly enough so that the listener has a chance to understand your message without your having to repeat it. Keep in mind that as you speak the other person may be taking notes.

Pronunciation is the correct way to say a word. To avoid mispronouncing words, you may wish to check pronunciation of unfamiliar words in the dictionary before you use them.

People with an accent unlike yours may not understand your pronunciation of some words. You also may not understand the pronunciation of some of their words. In these cases, careful pronunciation is very important for effective communication. You may need to repeat or spell words that are unusual or easy to be misunderstood.

1. When speaking on the phone, the essential factor for successful communication is your _____.
  A. voice B. gesture C. eye contact D. facial expression
2. To give important information, a person speaking on the phone should _____.
  A. keep a pleasant manner B. use familiar words
  C. lower the voice D. speak louder
3. The speaker is advised to speak slowly in order to help the listener to _____.
  A. remember some words B. repeat the information
  C. check the message D. take some notes
4. To avoid mispronouncing unfamiliar words, you are advised to _____.
  A. check them in a dictionary B. pronounce them loudly
  C. use other words instead D. ask others for help
5. Speakers sometimes need to spell some words to help listeners to understand _____.
  A. long sentences B. unusual words
  C. difficult questions D. important expressions

Task 2

Directions: *Read the following passage and make the correct choice.*

The first aid you learn from a course is not quite like reality. Most of us feel afraid when dealing with "the real thing." By overcoming these feelings, we are better able to use the first aid to cope with the unexpected.

Doing your part

First aid is not an exact science, and is thus open to human error. No matter how hard you try, the casualty may not respond as hoped. Some conditions might lead to death, even with the best medical care.

Giving care with confidence

The casualty needs to feel protected and in safe hands. You can create an air of confidence and safety by:

Being in control, both of yourself and the problem;

Acting calmly and reasonably;

Being gentle, but firm, with your hands, and speaking to the casualty kindly, but hopefully.

Building up trust

Talk to the casualty throughout your examination and treatment;

Explain what you are going to do;

Try to answer questions honestly to reduce fears as best as you can. If you do not know the answer, say so.

6. When we deal with the real cases of first aid, we often feel _____.

   A. safe   B. afraid   C. excited   D. confided

7. "First aid is … open to human error" in the second paragraph means _____.

   A. there are never failures in first aid

   B. medical care in first aid is essential

   C. human mistakes are possible in first aid

   D. first aid is widely applied to accidents

8. An air of confidence and safety is important in giving first aid because the casualty needs to feel to be _____.

   A. in control   B. comfortable

   C. in safe hands   D. gentle but firm

9. Which of the following can be a way to build up the casualty's trust?

   A. To answer their questions honestly.   B. To use as much medicine as possible.

   C. To avoid saying no to their questions.   D. To provide them with the best treatment.

10. The best title for the passage could be _____.

   A. Importance of Giving First Aid   B. Advice on Giving First Aid

   C. Future of First Aid   D. Types of First Aid

Task 3

Directions: *Read the following passage. After reading it, you should complete the information by filling in the blanks marked 11 to 15 (**in no more than 3 words**) in the table below. You should write your answers on the Answer Sheet correspondingly.*

Do you always understand directions on a bottle of medicine? Do you know what is meant by "Take only as directed?" Read the following directions and see if you understand them.

"To reduce pain, take two pills with water, followed by one pill every eight hours, as required. For night-time and early morning relief take two pills at bedtime. Do not take more than six pills in twenty-four hours.

For children six to twelve years old, give half the amount. For children under six years old, ask your doctor's advice.

Reduce the amount if you suffer from sleeplessness after taking the medicine.

During the first three months of *pregnancy* (妊娠) drugs should be used under the close direction of doctors. Drinking is advised to be forbidden.

The medicine will keep for five years if stored in a dry place at a temperature not above 25℃."

> Directions for Taking Medicine
> **Directions:** "Take only as directed" often appears on a ___11___.
> **Amount:** A 9-year-old child take at most ___12___ pills in twenty-four hours.
> If you can't sleep after taking the medicine, you should ___13___.
> **Cautions:** During taking the medicine, you are advised not to ___14___.
> **Storage:** The medicine should be stored at a temperature ___15___.

Task 4

Directions: *The following is a list of terms of trade (贸易术语). After reading it, you are required to find the items equivalent to (与……等同) those given in Chinese in the table below. Then you should mark the corresponding letters in order of the numbered blanks, 16 through 20 on the Answer Sheet.*

A—Price Term   J—Time of Shipment
B—Cost and Freight   K—Business Negotiation
C—Import License   L—Purchase Confirmation
D—Wholesale Price   M—Time of Delivery
E—Distribution Channel N—Free Trade Zone
F—Bonded Warehouse   O—Sales Commission
G—Favorable Balance of Trade   P—Net Price
H—Retail Price   Q—Customs Duty
I—Export Rebate

Examples: （ I ）出口退税   （ J ）装运时间
   16. （   ）贸易顺差   （   ）分销隧道
   17. （   ）自由贸易区   （   ）交易磋商
   18. （   ）进口许可证   （   ）销售提成
   19. （   ）价格条款   （   ）批发价
   20. （   ）购货确认书   （   ）交货时间

Task 5

Directions: *Read the following passage that is a letter of job application. After reading it, you are required to complete the answers that follow the questions. You should write your answers* **in no more than 3 words**.

Dear Sir/Madam,

  In response to your advertisement in yesterday's *Time Educational Supplement*, I would like to apply for the job of teaching English. I enclose a copy of my resume, a letter of recommendation from my current employer and copies of relevant certificates.

  As you will see from my resume, I have been teaching English to groups of adults of mixed nationalities in the past two years. I have taught students at all levels and I am experienced in preparing students for external exams. Though I have no experience of teaching children, I am sure that I would be able to adapt my understanding of teaching adults appropriately for children and quickly develop the relevant skills. I have always been able to learn new skills quite easily and I enjoy the challenge that each new experience represents. I feel certain that I could use my skills in ways that could benefit your organization. Please do not hesitate to contact me if you require my further information.

Yours faithfully,
Peter Garner

21. What position would the author like to apply for?

The author would like to apply for the job of _____.

22. What else does the author send to the employer besides his resume and recommendation letter?

He sends copies of _____ too.

23. What kind of students has the author once taught?

He has taught the students _____.

24. What experience does the author not have?

The author does not have the experience of _____.

25. According to the passage, what does the author enjoy from the new experience?

He enjoys _____ that the new experience represents.

Part Ⅲ Translation (English into Chinese)

1. Peter misunderstood the instructions his boss gave him and mailed the wrong documents to the supplier.

  A. 彼得按照老板给他的指示，把单据误寄给了供货商。

  B. 彼得误解了老板对他的指示，向供货商发错了单据。

  C. 彼得对老板的指示还没有理解就把错误的单据交给供货商。

2. I will give you a clear idea of the market conditions in the region as soon as possible.

A. 我会尽快地让你们清楚地了解该地区的市场情况。
B. 我会尽可能设法弄清该地区的市场销售情况。
C. 我会尽早向你们清楚地说明该地区的市场状况。

3. Congratulations on purchasing from our company the C800 Coffee Maker, which is suitable for home use.
A. 我公司隆重推出 C800 型家用咖啡壶，欢迎各界人士惠顾。
B. 您从我公司购买了最新款的 C800 型家用咖啡壶，值得祝贺。
C. 恭喜您购买本公司 C800 型咖啡壶，此款咖啡壶适合居家使用。

4. The function of e-commerce is more than just buying and selling goods and services on the Internet.
A. 电子商务的功能很多，如提供网上货物交易的服务。
B. 电子商务更多的功能在于做买卖并提供网络服务。
C. 电子商务的功能不只是在互联网上买卖货物和服务。

5. Now people have a choice about where they work and what kind of work they'll do. They are faced with the challenge of deciding where to go. They need to know what standard to use in making their decisions. This book provides them with practical advice for making their choices. Meanwhile, they will know what questions to ask, what jobs to look for, and how to make their final decisions.

_____
_____
_____
_____

Part Ⅳ Practical Writing

Directions: *This part is to test your ability to do practical writing. You are required to write an e-mail according to the information given below in Chinese. Remember to do your writing on the Translation/Composition Sheet.*

说明：假设你是 Hongxia Trading Company 的雇员王东，给客户 Mr. Baker 发一封电子邮件，内容如下：
1）欢迎他来福州；
2）告诉他已在东方宾馆为他预订了房间；
3）告诉他从国际机场到达东方宾馆大约 20 公里，可以乘坐出租车或机场大巴；
4）建议他第二天来你的办公室洽谈业务；

5）如需帮助，请电话联系。

Word for reference: 机场大巴 shuttle bus

An E-mail

Dear Mr. Baker,

Supplementary Reading

Passage A

Nature's Spring Miracle　春天的奇迹

Those tough little crocuses poking through the snow proved to my family that we could survive anything.	顽强的娇小的番红花破雪而出昭示着我们可以战胜任何艰难困苦。
Winter was a new experience after we moved to the farm from Black Lake.	我们从黑湖搬到农场以后，冬天给了我们一种全新的体验。
It seemed colder, longer, and more isolating. We couldn't run across the street to meet our friends for a day of ice skating or sledding. There was no large group of kids to play with as we waited for the school bus. Our closest neighbors were now a quarter of a mile away.	那里的冬天似乎更加漫长而寒冷，也显得更加孤寂。因为我们不能再跑过大街，和我们的伙伴一起滑冰或者滑雪橇。在我们等候校车之时，不再有大群的孩子在一起玩耍。最近的邻居也在1/4英里以外。

My brother and sister and I waited alone in the cold at the top of our driveway for the school bus. We did have hills to slide on, but no lake for skating or fishing—the closest ice rink was five miles away in Carver.

The first winter we spent at the farm was especially difficult.

My mother developed pneumonia at Christmas time, and it took her a long while to recover.

Minnesota winters can be brutal and I remember that one as especially cold. There were short episodes of being snowed in, waiting for several days for the county plows to get to our little road. We all went a bit stir crazy and were more than ready for spring.

March finally rolled around. The snow was melting and on days when the sun was shining the air hinted at warmer weather. But March was a capricious month.

One day the breeze would be warm and balmy and you might even catch sight of a robin, the next it would be gray and threatening snow.

One Sunday afternoon while my father was trying to nap, my siblings and I were encouraged to go for a hike.

我们兄弟姐妹只能一起在寒冷的冬日里孤单地站在车道尽头等校车。我们可以在山上滑雪，但是不能滑冰或钓鱼，因为附近没有湖。距我们最近的滑冰场在五英里以外的卡弗。

我们在农场度过的第一个冬天异常艰难。

我的妈妈在圣诞节期间患上了肺炎，过了许久，方才康复。

明尼苏达州的冬天异常难熬，而那一年的冬天的严寒让我至今记忆犹新。连续数日大雪封门，只能耐心等待来自县城的爬犁到达我们农场。我们都焦躁不安，几近疯狂，更加热切盼望春天的到来。

时光荏苒，三月终于到来了。积雪渐渐消融，阳光普照的日子，天气暖意融融。但三月的天气反复无常，让人捉摸不定。

头一天还是暖风拂面，甚至都能看到知更鸟的身影，第二天却是天空灰暗，风雪交加。

一个周日下午，爸爸准备小睡片刻，他鼓励我们兄弟姐妹去远足。我们决定直抵桦树山。那原本是一条可以让

We decided on Birch Hill as our destination. It was far enough away to keep us out of doors for several hours, but not such a lengthy walk that Cass, my six-year-old sister, would get tired halfway there.

Things were a bit wet and muddy, but most of the snow was gone.

We started off through the open alfalfa field, making our way to the adjoining meadow. The sun shone with the soft light of spring, making everything seem muted and fuzzy around the edges. Fluffy white clouds were scattered across the pale blue sky.

A slight breeze ruffled our hair, now free of winter's wool stocking caps. We could see the faintest hint of green beneath last year's dead meadow grass and buds were just beginning to swell on the red dogwood branches. Bird songs filled the air and everything smelled of new life.

We had never before paid attention to the all of the changes spring brings. The meadow sloped gently upwards, rising gradually, and suddenly the bright white trunks of the birch trees were visible.

The small grove of white paper birch looked slightly out of place, almost as though the trees had been

我们足足走上几个小时的漫长之旅，但我们悠然自得，信步前行，即便连六岁的小妹卡斯在中途也没有感到劳累。

地面略显潮湿而泥泞，但是积雪大多已不见踪迹。

我们穿过空旷的紫花苜蓿田，一路向前，来到与之毗邻的草地。和煦的春光暖暖地照着大地，四周一片静谧而朦胧。懒散的白云在淡蓝色的天空飘荡。

摘掉了冬天的羊毛帽子，微风吹拂着我们的头发。我们依稀可辨去年已经干枯的草地里泛出来的些许绿意以及红瑞木枝条上刚刚发出的嫩芽正在一点点地舒展。到处充盈着欢快的鸟鸣，到处弥漫着新生的气息。

我们以往从未注意到春天会带来如此巨大的变化。沿着平缓的草坡漫步而上，闪亮的白桦树干突然映入我们的眼帘。

只是那一小片白色的纸皮桦林看起来有些扎眼，似乎是被有意栽种在那儿的。因为除此之外，你再也找不到其

intentionally planted there. No other birch trees could be found anywhere else on the property, just this small grove in the midst of cotton woods, oaks, and elms.

他白桦树的影子。而满眼看到的只是大片的异叶杨、橡树和榆树林。

As we approached the grove it appeared as though there were purple balls scattered beneath the trees, even on top of the patches of snow, but upon closer inspection we realized the purple balls were actually flowers—tiny, velvet, upside down purple balls carpeted the ground beneath the trees.

当我们走近白桦林时，忽然发现树下遍布着紫色的小球，甚至在片片残雪之上也隐约可见。行至跟前，我们却吃惊地发现，那些紫色的小球竟然是怒放的花朵——娇小的，天鹅绒般的，羞涩地低着头，在树下铺成了紫色的地毯。

We were amazed. We had never seen flowers in the snow.

我们惊诧不已，从未见过能傲雪绽放的花朵。

My little sister immediately wanted to pick some to take to my mother.

我的小妹情不自禁，欲伸手摘花，送给妈妈。

"No," I said, "Let's bring mother here. Let's surprise her with the first spring flowers!"

"不要那样。"我阻止了她，"为何不带妈妈来这儿，让她亲自感受早春之花所带来的惊喜呢！"

My brother and sister agreed this was a good idea. We hurried back home as fast as we could through the final remnants of snow, last year's soggy grass, and the muddy field.

兄弟姐妹一致赞成。于是我们转过身来，踏过最后的残雪，穿过萧瑟的枯草，踩过泥泞的田野，飞也似的跑回家。

When we arrived, we excitedly told our mother that we had a surprise to show her. We knew that mother would have excuses so we let Cass do the begging since she was the baby of the family.

我们一到家，就兴奋地告诉妈妈我们要给她一个惊喜。唯恐妈妈会找各种理由拒绝，我们便让家中最小的孩子卡斯恳求妈妈随我们一同前往。

After much cajoling, my mother reluctantly agreed. She pulled on her ratty old winter car coat and her black rubber boots and off we went. It wasn't easy trying to hurry through the mud in the alfalfa field, but soon we were in the meadow and approaching Birch Hill.

When my mother saw the flowers, she just stopped and stared, then let out a quiet awestruck "oohh."

Saying nothing, she began to walk very carefully beneath the trees looking at the tiny flowers. We followed silently in her footsteps. It felt like we were in church.

"What are they, Mama?" Cass asked in a near whisper.

"They're crocuses," my mother answered softly, "tough little flowers that will bloom even in the snow— nature's spring miracle."

It was then I noticed tears glistening on my mother's cheeks.

"Are you OK, Mama?" I asked a little worried.

"Yes, honey," she answered smiling, "I'm just so very happy you shared this special surprise with me."

一番甜言蜜语后,妈妈不情愿地同意了。她穿上破旧的短大衣和黑胶靴。我们便一同上路。我们费了好大劲儿才匆忙地走过泥泞的苜蓿田,来到宽阔的草地,接近桦树山。

当妈妈一看到那些小花,便停下脚步,瞪大眼睛,发出一声惊叹。

她一语不发,小心翼翼地在树下漫步,注视着那些娇小的花朵。我们也静静地紧随其后,仿佛在教堂一样。

"它们是什么花?"卡斯小声地问道。

"它们是番红花,"妈妈轻声回答,"顽强的小花竟会傲雪绽放,这是大自然里春天的奇迹。"

恰在此时,我看到妈妈的面颊上闪着晶莹的泪光。

"你没事吧?"我略有担忧地问。

"没事,宝贝。"妈妈微笑着说,"我真的很高兴你们能和我一起分享这个惊喜。"

From that point on, a pilgrimage to find the crocuses became a yearly rite of spring until I grew up and moved away.	从那时起,每年春天观赏番红花已经成为我们家的盛事,直到我长大成人,离开农场。
Sometimes we all went together, sometimes my mother went alone or I did, especially during moody adolescence, but each year we eagerly awaited that first miracle of the season.	有时我们全家集体出动,有时则是妈妈或我单独前往,特别是在我青春萌动、情绪不稳之时。但是不管怎样,我们每年都急切地盼望着春天带给我们的第一个奇迹。

Passage B

Validation 抉择

I was probably one of the few kids in America whose parents didn't want her to go to college. It's not that they didn't want me to go, exactly, now that I look back at it, but, just as everything else in high school, there was the major issue of money.	在美国,很少有父母不想让孩子上大学,可我就是这些孩子中的一员。确切地说,并不是父母真的不想让我上大学。如今回想起来,就像我在高中时所遭遇的其他所有事情一样,主要还是钱的问题。
My family is very blue collar. My parents started having kids very young, and I felt they were never able to achieve more than getting a factory job, and trying to make ends meet as their family grew.	我生活在极普通的工人家庭。我的父母很早就开始生儿育女。我感觉他们最大的成就,也就是找到一份工厂的工作,并随着家庭成员的增加努力维持收支平衡。
While I was growing up, it was fine to speak in theoretical terms about going to college. I would always say I wanted to go to an Ivy League school and then practice neurosurgery at the Mayo Clinic, and my dad would say there was absolutely nothing wrong with our state university. My aunt Mary, the only person in both extended families to go to school before me, had gone	随着我一天天长大,理论上说,谈论上大学的事情顺理成章。我总会说我想要去一所常春藤大学就读,然后去梅奥医学中心当一名神经外科医生。爸爸也总是说我们州立大学绝对没什么问题。姑姑玛丽是父母双方家族中在我之前唯一上过大学的人。她念的就是州立大学。如今是一位赫赫有名的律

there and she was a big-shot lawyer taking in loads of money. So Dad suggested that's what I ought to shoot for.

The one thing I vividly remembered hating in high school was asking for money. When my junior year arrived, I had signed up for the whole course load of Advanced Placement classes. Even though the AP tests were only $22 at that time, my mom would question why I needed the money and, I believe, huff a little bit as she wrote out the check. I gave creative speeches about how much AP would save me at college, and that those $22 would be parlayed into thousands of dollars of tuition money.

By the time senior year rolled around, I sent out only two applications for college, one to the state university a little more than two hours away from my hometown, and one to a school in another state. I was quickly accepted into both, but this was the point at which I felt somewhat blindsided by my parents. My dad, at least, seemed to be against the idea of my going away for school. He wanted me to attend the extension in our county and save money by continuing to live at home.

The mere thought of staying home another two years was enough to turn my stomach. I was already attending some classes at "The Stench," because my high school didn't offer the accelerated classes I qualified for. Although it was a fine school, and many people did transfer from the

师，收入颇丰。因此，爸爸认为那就是我应当为之奋斗的目标。

我清楚地记得，高中时一直痛恨的一件事情是向父母要钱。我升入高二年级时，报名参加了包含所有课程的大学先修班。尽管那时该班的测试费仅有22美元。但妈妈还是会质疑我为什么需要那些钱，并且我确信，妈妈在填写支票时还有点生气。我多次颇有创意地发表演说：大学先修课程能让我在大学里省下多大一笔银子。而那22美元则将会增值为成千上万的学费。

到上高三的时候，我只发出了两份大学申请书；一份发给了离我的家乡两个多小时车程的州立大学，另一份则发给了别的州的一所学校。很快我就被两所院校同时录取。但是恰在这一点上，父母令我感到有些吃惊。至少爸爸看起来似乎反对我离家求学的想法。他想让我在本县的进修部继续求学，并想让我继续住在家里来节省开支。

仅仅只是想到自己还要在家待上两年，我便会感到厌烦。我已经在上那所"烂校"的一些课程了，因为我所在的高中没开设适合我学习的快班。尽管那是一所好学校，并且许多人还确实从这所进修部转到了州里的主校区，但我知道

extension to the main state school, I knew I wouldn't follow that path.

For whatever reason, I had been given more ambition than my parents before me, or my two younger brothers, both of whom opted for the factory scene rather than education. But I could see this ambition having an ending point, as if it were mistakenly siphoned into me and would be sucked out if I spent too much time in my small town. I could see in my mind's eye how discouraged I would get living at home for two more years under my parents' ironclad rule, either getting frustrated at the extension, or finding more value in the attention from boys, ending up pregnant and working at the nearby gas station. Not my idea of a future.

So every day after school, my dad and I had blown out fights about where I would go to college. His logic was very sound, especially considering where I stand now, three years after graduation with debt up to my eyeballs, but I just knew I would get nowhere staying in my hometown. He threatened to give me no financial help at all, and I said that was fine, I would be able to get enough loans.

Eventually I signed my family up for a tour of the state university. My dad and I toured campus, and even though it was so cold, my dad fell in love—or at the very least seemed very enthusiastic about every corner of the campus.

我不会那么做。

无论什么原因，与我的父母以及宁愿选择工厂也不愿接受教育的两个弟弟相比，我已被赋予了更远大的抱负。但是我能看到这个抱负有一个终结点，仿佛它被错误地注入我的心中，而如果我在家乡小镇耗费太多时间，它就会被吸空。在内心深处我可以看到，如果我在父母严苛的管教下再在家里住上两年，我会变得多么沮丧：要么会对这个进修部灰心，要么会从男孩子们的关注中找到更多的自我价值，最终结婚生子，在附近的加油站工作。这可不是我对未来的想法。

这样一来，每天放学后我和爸爸就会为我去哪儿上大学而爆发争吵。他的逻辑非常合理，尤其是考虑到我当前的处境——高中毕业后三年之内，我将债台高筑。但是我深知待在家乡我将一事无成。他威胁说不给我任何经济支持，我回答说没关系，我会得到足够的贷款。

最终我给全家报了名去参加州立大学观光游。我和爸爸游览了整个校园，尽管天气很冷，爸爸还是很快就喜欢上了这所学校——或者至少看上去对这所学校的每一个角落都热情有加。

I could tell he was softened by this visit, but the fights about where I was going to get the money continued until the day I packed everything up into our minivan. It was then, at breakfast before we made our journey down, that my dad said he was proud of me. He hadn't thought I would actually leave, and he was impressed. As my parents dropped me off at my dorm room, my mom started crying hysterically, and even my dad teared up, kissing me on the forehead, which was the first time I could remember getting hugged and kissed by them in years.

At this point, my relationship with my parents changed. No longer were they the disciplinarians, but they became confidants, advisors and an excellent support system, and I became an adult. Sometimes I still expect to get yelled at for my decisions, but they've done phenomenally well to leave me to my own life, and to just be happy when I actually call home. No matter what happens now, I know standing my ground on where to go for school has been the best decision of my life, as I have gained both a good education and a precious life experience I never would have been exposed to had I taken any other road.

我能断定通过这次参观，他的态度软化了。但是关于我将去哪儿筹到钱的争吵却仍在继续，直到我将所有用品都打包装进我家的小货车里。就在我们上路前吃早餐的时候，爸爸说他以我为荣。他没有想到我会真的离家远行，他深受感动。当父母驱车把我送到宿舍时，妈妈开始歇斯底里地大哭起来，就连爸爸眼里也泛起了泪花。他们亲吻了我的额头。这可是数年来我能记起的第一次被他们拥抱和亲吻。

就在这一刻，我和父母的关系改变了。他们不再是严师，反而成了我的密友、顾问以及坚强后盾。我也变成了成年人。有时我还期盼能够因为我的决定而受到他们的责骂，但是他们已经能坦然面对，任由我安排自己的人生。当我给家里打电话的时候，他们都很高兴。无论现在情况如何，我知道为去哪儿上大学而坚持到底是我人生中最棒的一个决定。因为我不仅得到了良好的教育，还拥有了一次宝贵的人生体验。——假如我选择了其他的人生道路，这些我将永远都不会拥有。

Unit Eight

Part I Vocabulary & Structure

Section A

Directions: *In this section, there are 10 incomplete sentences. You are required to complete each one by deciding on the most appropriate word or words from the 4 choices marked A, B, C and D. Then you should mark the corresponding letter on the Answer Sheet with a single line through the center.*

1. Do not _____ me to help you unless you work harder.
   A. expect	B. hope	C. depend	D. think
2. The question _____ now is where to build the new factory.
   A. discusses	B. discussing
   C. be discussed	D. being discussed
3. John decided to _____ the present job in order to travel around the world.
   A. give up	B. put up	C. wake up	D. break up
4. Michael's new house looks like a palace, compared _____ his old one.
   A. of	B. with	C. for	D. in
5. Computer technology makes it _____ for people to work from home.
   A. harmful	B. serious	C. possible	D. difficult
6. We are delighted at the news _____ they have started the business cooperation with your company.
   A. that	B. when	C. which	D. what
7. The computer program is designed for the _____ of easy online reading.
   A. experience	B. purpose	C. invitation	D. decision
8. The business talk _____ next week when the CEO of your company comes.
   A. was held	B. being held
   C. will be held	D. has been held
9. It was so noisy that we found it hard to _____ the conversation.
   A. carry on	B. set for	C. turn on	D. go about
10. You can't cancel your order _____ you change your mind within three days.

A. as if   B. while   C. so that   D. unless

Section B

Directions: *There are 5 incomplete statements here. You should fill in each blank with the proper form of the word given in brackets. Write the word or words in the corresponding space on the Answer Sheet.*

11. Jack (quick) _____ established himself as a powerful member of the new company.

12. When she got back from the South, Susan had her car (wash) _____ thoroughly.

13. We all like your idea of using the money (build) _____ a primary school.

14. She wants to apply for a new job as her present job is not (interest) _____.

15. The UK economy last year performed (well) _____ than expected according to the report.

Part Ⅱ Reading Comprehension

Task 1

Directions: *Read the following passage and make the correct choice.*

A car is made up of more than 30,000 parts. Each part in a new car is as weak as a baby. So a new car requires proper care and servicing. If you're unfamiliar with the parts, you have to read through the owner's instructions carefully.

First of all, the brakes of your car are important for safety reason. Having them checked regularly can reduce the risks of accidents. Another important thing to consider is engine care. Always remember that the life and performance of your car engine depend on the engine oil. Replace the engine oil when recommended. If you feel the engine is very hot especially during summer, it is probably because the cooling system doesn't work well. You'd better get the cooling system service before the start of summer.

In a word, timely and proper servicing is an important task for car owners. Good servicing can not only extend the life of your newborn baby, but also ensure your safety, and the safety of those who share the road with you.

1. To get familiar with the parts of a new car, the owner should _____.

    A. regard the car as a new-born baby

    B. have the car serviced before driving it

    C. read through the instructions carefully

   D. examine all of the parts of the new car
  2. The brakes should be checked regularly _____.
   A. to avoid accidents   B. to raise speed
   C. to reduce cost   D. to save gas
  3. For a car engine to work long and well, the owner should _____.
   A. replace the engine oil as recommended
   B. reduce the use of the car in summer
   C. clean the engine parts regularly
   D. change the brakes frequently
  4. It is recommended to have the cooling system checked when _____.
   A. you buy a new car   B. summer is coming
   C. the engine oil is replaced D. the brakes are out of order
  5. The last paragraph tells us that the purpose of carefully servicing a car is_____.
   A. to let you sell your car at a good price
   B. to extend its life and ensure safety
   C. to reduce the cost of car servicing
   D. to make the car run faster

Task 2

Directions: *Read the following passage and make the correct choice.*

Ticket-booking policies

General Policies
★ Once the flight ticket has been issued, the name on the ticket cannot be changed.
★ Ticket is non-refundable.
★ Please review your itinerary immediately. If any problems arise before or during your trip, you must call our booking offices right away. If you wait until return, it's too late.
★ There are times when we are unable to confirm a booking. In that case we will attempt to reach you by phone and e-mail. You must call us back within 48 hours or we may not be able to offer you the booking price.

Change Policies
★ If you change your booking, airlines may charge a fee—$150 to $200.
★ Some tickets do not allow any changes.
Need to change or cancel your trip? Visit our website to check the fees and rules before you decide.

Cancellation (取消) Policies

★ If you cancel your booking you will not receive any money back.

★ You may apply part of your ticket price towards future travel (for a limited time, usually a year).

6. According to the policies, the name on the ticket cannot be changed once the ticket is _____.

    A. booked   B. issued   C. cancelled   D. confirmed

7. If you have any problems during a trip, you should _____.

    A. ask for refund   B. change your itinerary

    C. call the booking office   D. return the ticket to the office

8. What happens when your ticket booking cannot be confirmed?

    A. You should make another booking immediately.

    B. You can change your booking free of charge.

    C. You will be informed by phone and e-mail.

    D. You will still enjoy the booking price.

9. If you want to change a booking, you may have to pay _____.

    A. 10% of the booking price   B. a fee of $150 to $200

    C. half the ticket price   D. a fixed fee

10. Which of the following statements is TRUE according to the cancellation policies?

    A. You can use part of the ticket price for future travel.

    B. You can refund the money from the booking office.

    C. You can keep the booking effective for one year.

    D. You cannot cancel your booking in any case.

Task 3

Directions: *The following is the safety instructions of a brand of colorant gel. After reading it, you should complete the information by filling in the blanks marked 11 through 15* **(in no more than 3 words)** *in the table below. You should write the answers on the Answer Sheet correspondingly.*

Read before Use

Important: This product can cause an allergic reaction(过敏反应) which, in rare cases, may be severe. To help you reduce the risk of allergic reactions, it is essential to follow the precautions (注意事项) below:

1. Skin test

Perform a skin test 48 hours before using this product, even if you have already used a hair colorant (染发剂) of this or any other brands before.

2. In case of a reaction during the application, rinse (冲洗) immediately with lukewarm (微温的) water. Stop using the product, and before coloring your hair again, consult a doctor:

Avoid contact with eyes.

Rinse eyes immediately if the product comes into contact with them.

Wear suitable gloves supplied in the package.

Do not use it to color eyelashes and eyebrows or for any purpose other than coloring the hair.

Keep out of the reach of children.

Safety Instructions

To be safe, you'd better test skin ___11___ before using the product.

Some of the SHOULD-NOTS about this product:

1. If there is any kind of reaction, you should rinse your hair immediately with ___12___.
2. You should not make the product get into your eyes.
3. While using the product, you should wear ___13___.
4. You should not use the product to color ___14___.
5. You should keep the product away from ___15___.

Task 4

Directions: *The following is a list of trade terms. After reading it, you are required to find the items equivalent to (与……等同) those given in Chinese in the table below. Then you should mark the corresponding letters in order of the numbered blanks, 16 through 20 on the Answer Sheet.*

A—Economic Giant
B—Economic Means
C—Economic Liftoff
D—Economic Depression
E—Economic Efficiency
F—Economic Integration
G—Economic Index

J—Trade Companion
K—Business Machine
L—Business Interest
M—Shopping Center
N—Business World
O—Spot Exchange
P—Regional Economy

H—Trade Gap   Q—Commodity Economy
I—Trade Agreement

Example: （B）经济手段   （M）商业区
16.（ ）经济腾飞   （ ）贸易协定
17.（ ）现货交易   （ ）经济指数
18.（ ）经济一体化   （ ）商业利益
19.（ ）经济萧条   （ ）贸易逆差
20.（ ）区域经济   （ ）经济大国

Task 5

Directions: There is a business letter here. After reading it, you are required to complete the answers that follow the questions. You should write your answers **in no more than 3 words**.

Dear Sirs,

　　We have heard from China Council (委员会) for the Promotion of International Trade that you are in the market for silk garments (服装).

　　We are introducing ourselves as one of the leading exporters of the same business line. And we would like to establish relations with you on the basis of equality, mutual benefit and the exchange of needed goods.

　　Our silk garments are made of super pure silk materials and with traditional skills. They are magnificent and tasteful and have long enjoyed a great fame both at home and abroad. We enclose a catalog for your reference and trust some of these items will be of interest to you.

　　We would be very much interested in receiving your inquiries and sending you our quotations (价目表).

　　We look forward to your favorable reply.

　　　　　　　　　　　　　　　　　　　　　　　　Yours faithfully,
　　　　　　　　　　　　　　　　　　　　　　　　Tom Green

21. What is the full name of China Council mentioned by the writer?
    China Council for the Promotion of _____.
22. How does the writer make the self-introduction?
    One of the _____ in the market for silk garments.
23. What kind of materials are the garments made of?
    _____.
24. How are the silk garments made?
    Our silk garments are made with _____.

25. What else does the writer enclose with the letter?

_____ for his reference.

Part Ⅲ   Translation (English into Chinese)

1. It seems that women are more attracted to the convenience of online shopping than they used to be.

    A. 看起来网上购物更加容易了，现在比过去更能吸引现代女性。

    B. 现代的妇女与传统的妇女比较起来，似乎更加喜欢网络购物。

    C. 看起来，如今的妇女比起过去更加为网络购物的便捷所吸引。

2. We have played an important role in helping these companies to establish a strong network platform.

    A. 我们在帮助这些公司建立起强大的网络平台方面发挥出了重要作用。

    B. 我们能帮助这些公司建立强大的网络平台，并可以做出重大的贡献。

    C. 我们对这些网络公司的帮助是巨大的，并为他们的发展提供了平台。

3. If anything should go wrong with your computer, refer all servicing to qualified service personnel.

    A. 如果你不会使用这台计算机，务必向专业人士进行咨询。

    B. 你的计算机出现任何毛病，都得找合格的维修人员维修。

    C. 你的计算机出了问题，请按此地址与维修人员进行联系。

4. The new system, which should be in use by the end of this month, will replace the current one.

    A. 新系统在本月月底以前应该启用，以取代现有的系统。

    B. 已经启用的新系统将从本月底开始替换现有的系统。

    C. 本月月底已经完成全部新系统的安装和旧系统的维护。

5. It's our responsibility to provide our staff with the best technical support services. We are working hard to give clear information about each of the services we provide. And we also aim to achieve the highest service standards. However, please remember that things can sometimes go wrong. If this happens, please let us know right away by calling 01782294443. We will do everything we can to put things right.

Part IV Practical Writing

Directions: *This part is to test your ability to do practical writing. You are required to write a paragraph according to the information given below in Chinese. Remember to do your writing on Translation/Composition Sheet.*

1. 我们可以给亲朋好友发电子邮件，打电话。
2. 我们也可以上网络学校，阅读各种书籍，自学外语。
3. 我们还可以欣赏音乐，观看体育比赛，玩电脑游戏，网上购物，这丰富了我们的生活。

Supplementary Reading

Passage A

Only Words 慎用你的语言

My father is a triathlete. That is, he has competed in several triathlons—a kind of marathon that includes running as well as swimming and bike riding. He's been doing it for years, and he really enjoys all the sports, but his favorite is bike riding. Ever since I was little, I've always loved going biking with my dad. We would leave the city behind and follow the bike trails way up into	我的爸爸是一名铁人三项运动员。他曾参加过几次铁人三项比赛——一种包括长跑、游泳以及自行车骑行在内的马拉松运动。多年来他一直坚持这项运动。对这三种运动他都乐此不疲。但他最喜爱的还是骑自行车。自打我小时候起，我总是愿意与爸爸一起骑自行车锻炼。我们会把城市远远地甩在身

the woods of Wisconsin. We had a favorite spot where we would picnic. It was always our special time, and it kept me in great physical shape.

But as I grew older and became a teenager, I was distracted by other things to do with my time. Suddenly, it was very important to go shopping with friends or to a movie with a boy. I saw my dad every evening at home.

If my indifference hurt him, he never let on. He never asked me outright, but would always let me know when he was planning a bike trip in case I wanted to come.

I didn't, and as I approached my sixteenth birthday, I wanted to spend less and less time with my dad. Except for one thing—I didn't mind being with him when he was giving me a driving lesson.

More than anything else, I wanted that driver's license. It meant freedom. It meant no more waiting for parents to pick me up. No more carpools. It meant looking cool behind the wheel of a car as I drove past my friends' houses. Of course, since I didn't have my own car, I would still be dependent on my parents, since they were allowing me to use theirs.

It was a Sunday morning, and I was in a terrible mood. Two of my friends had gone to the movies the night before and hadn't

后，一路骑行，来到威斯康星林间。在那儿有一个我们最爱去野餐的地方。一起骑行总是我们最快乐的时光，同时也使我身体健壮。

但是随着我一天天长大，成为一名青少年。我便忙于用别的事情来打发我的时间。不知不觉间与朋友逛街，与男孩子看电影变得十分重要。只有每天晚上回到家，我才能看到爸爸。

即便我的淡漠伤害了他，他却没流露出丝毫的不快。他从没直接问过我，但每次他计划骑车出游时总会告诉我一声，以免万一我也想同去而错过。

而事实上我却不想去。随着我日渐接近16岁的生日，我愿意陪爸爸的时间越来越少。只有一件事除外——那就是爸爸教我开车的时候，我并不介意与他共处。

与其他任何事情相比，我更想得到的是驾照。有了它，就意味着自由，意味着不用等父母接送或与他人拼车。意味着当我驾车驶过朋友家房前时看上去是那样的潇洒。当然，由于我没有自己的车，我仍然要依靠我的父母，因为他们允许我使用他们的车。

那是一个周日的早晨，我的心情糟糕极了。因为我的两个朋友头天晚上去看了电影，却没有邀请

invited me. I was in my room thinking of ways to make them sorry when my father poked his head in. "Want to go for a ride, today, Beck? It's a beautiful day."

But I preferred to sit in my room and stew. I wasn't very polite when I said, "No! Please stop asking me!" "Leave me alone!" Those were the last words I said to him before he left the house that morning.

My friends called and invited me to go to the mall with them a few hours later. I forgot to be mad at them and went.

I came home to find a note on the table. "Dad has had an accident. Please meet us at Highland Park Hospital. Don't hurry, just drive carefully. The keys are in the drawer."

I grabbed the keys and tried hard not to speed or cry as I drove.

When I reached the hospital, I went in through the emergency room. I remembered the way because I had been there once before when I broke my arm. I thought about that incident now. I had fallen out of the apple tree in our backyard. I started to scream, but before the scream was out of my mouth, there was my dad, scooping me up, holding me and my injured arm. He held me while my mother drove us to the emergency room. And he held me as they set my arm and put a pink cast on it. I do remember the pain, but I also remember how safe I felt in

我。我正待在房间里想办法怎么让他们感到歉疚。爸爸把头探进来，问道，"贝基，想出去骑车吗？天气真不错。"

但是我更愿待在自己的房间里怄气。我很不礼貌地回答，"不！不要再来问我！""让我独自待会儿。"这些就是那天上午爸爸离家前我最后对他所说的话。

几个小时后我的朋友们打来电话邀我同去购物中心。我早忘记了对他们的不满，欣然前往。

回家以后，我发现桌子上放着一张便条。"爸爸出车祸了。请到海兰德公园医院。不要太着急，开车一定要小心。钥匙在抽屉里。"

我抓起钥匙，驾车上路。我尽力控制自己，不要超速，不要哭泣。

当我到达医院时，我径直冲进急救室。我熟门熟路，因为以前我摔断胳膊，曾经来过这里。现在我想起了那次事故。我从我家后院的苹果树上掉了下来。我痛得想要大叫，可是还未来得及叫出声，爸爸就把我抱了起来，搂住我和那条伤臂。他抱着我，妈妈开车把我们送到急诊室，尔后他又抱住我让医生们固定我的胳膊，并打上粉色的石膏。至今那种疼痛依然记忆犹新，但是我仍然记得躺在爸爸强壮的臂弯里感觉多么安全。我也记得后

my dad's strong arms. And I remember the chocolate ice cream afterward.

I saw my sister Debbie first. She told me our mom was in with our dad and that he was going up to surgery soon. She said I had to wait to see him until after the surgery.

So I waited anxiously until the next afternoon. When I was allowed to see him, he was in terrible pain. I tried to tell him how sorry I was, but I couldn't tell if he heard me.

It was several days later that he was finally able to have a conversation. I held his hand gently, afraid of hurting him.

"Daddy... I am so sorry..."

"It's okay, sweetheart. I'll be Okay."

"No," I said, "I mean about what I said to you that day. You know, that morning?"

My father could no more tell a lie than he could fly. He looked at me blankly and said, "Sweetheart, I don't remember anything about that day, not before, during or after the accident. I remember kissing you goodnight the night before, though." He managed a weak smile.

I never wanted him to leave me alone.

来的巧克力冰淇淋。

我先是看到了我的姐姐黛比。她告诉我妈妈正在里面陪着爸爸，爸爸马上就要做手术了。姐姐说我必须等到手术后才能见到爸爸。

因此我只能焦急地一直等到第二天下午。当我被允许去探望爸爸的时候，他正遭受着剧痛的折磨。我尽力向他表达我的愧疚，但我却不能确定他是否能听到我的倾诉。

直到几天以后，他才能开口讲话。我轻握着他的手，以免伤到他。

"爸爸……我非常难过……"

"没什么，宝贝儿。我会好起来的。"

"不，"我说，"我是指那天我对您说的话。您还记得那天早晨吗？"

我的爸爸绝对不会撒谎。他茫然地看着我说道，"宝贝儿，那天发生的事我什么都不记得了，包括整个车祸前前后后。但是我记得前一天晚上我吻了你，并道晚安的情景。"他尽力露出了一丝笑容。

我永远不想让他把我独自留

And to think it might have happened. If he had been killed, we all would have been left alone. It was too horrible to imagine. I felt incredible remorse for my thoughtless remark.

I still remember my English teacher, a very wise woman, once told me that words have immeasurable power. They can hurt or they can heal. And we all have the power to choose our words. I intend to do that very carefully from now on.

Passage B

What Do You Value Most?

It had been some time since Jack had seen the old man. College, girls, career, and life itself got in the way. In fact, Jack moved clear across the country in pursuit of his dreams. There, in the rush of his busy life, Jack had little time to think about the past and often no time to spend with his wife and son. He was working on his future, and nothing could stop him.

Over the phone, his mother told him, "Mr. Belser died last night. The funeral is Wednesday." Memories flashed through his mind like an old newsreel as he sat quietly remembering his childhood days.

"Jack, did you hear me?"

"Oh, sorry, Mom. Yes, I heard you. It's been so long since I thought of him. I'm sorry, but I honestly thought he died years ago," Jack said.

"Well, he didn't forget you. Every time I saw him he'd ask how you were doing. He'd reminisce about the many days you spent over 'his side of the fence' as he put it," Mom told him.

"I loved that old house he lived in," Jack said.

"You know, Jack, after your father died, Mr. Belser stepped in to make sure you had a man's influence in your life," she said.

"He's the one who taught me carpentry," he said. "I wouldn't be in this business if it weren't for him. He spent a lot of time teaching me things he thought were important...Mom, I'll be there for the funeral," Jack said.

As busy as he was, he kept his word. Jack caught the next flight to his hometown.

Mr. Belser's funeral was small and uneventful. He had no children of his own, and most of his relatives had passed away.

The night before he had to return home, Jack and his mom stopped by to see the old house next door one more time.

Standing in the doorway, Jack paused for a moment. It was like crossing over into

几年前就不在了。"杰克说。

"不过，他倒没有忘记你。每次我见到他，他都向我询问你的近况如何。他还会忆起如其所言你在他家院子里度过的许多时光。"妈妈告诉杰克。

"我喜欢他居住的那所老房子。"杰克说。

"杰克，你知道，在你父亲去世之后，贝尔瑟先生便施以援手帮助我们，确保在你生活中受到男子汉的影响。"妈妈说。

"他是教我木工手艺的师傅。"杰克说："若不是因为他的缘故，我不会干这一行。他花费大量的时间来教给我他认为重要的东西……妈妈，我将会参加葬礼。"杰克说。

尽管他工作很忙，他还是如约前往。杰克搭乘最近的航班回到了家乡。

贝尔瑟先生的葬礼规模很小，进行得很顺利。他无儿无女，而且绝大多数亲属也已辞世。

在杰克必须返回自家的头天晚上，他和妈妈又一次去看了看隔壁那所老房子。

杰克站在门口，稍停片刻，感觉好像时空跳跃，进入了另一

another dimension, a leap through space and time.

The house was exactly as he remembered. Every step held memories. Every picture, every piece of furniture...Jack stopped suddenly.

"What's wrong, Jack?" his mom asked.

"The box is gone," he said.

"What box?" Mom asked.

"There was a small gold box that he kept locked on top of his desk. I must have asked him a thousand times what was inside. All he'd ever tell me was 'the thing I value most,'" Jack said.

It was gone. Everything about the house was exactly how Jack remembered it, except for the box. He figured someone from the Belser family had taken it.

"Now I'll never know what was so valuable to him," Jack said. "I better get some sleep. I have an early flight home, Mom."

It had been about two weeks since Mr. Belser died. Returning home from work one day Jack discovered a note in his mailbox.

"Signature required on a package. No one at home. Please stop by the main post

个空间。

这所房子和他记忆中的一模一样。每走一步就唤起不同的回忆。杰克审视着每张照片，每件家具……突然他停了下来。

"怎么了，杰克？"妈妈问道。

"那个盒子没了。"杰克答道。

"什么盒子？"妈妈问道。

"在桌子上有一个锁着的金色小盒子。我敢肯定曾问过他无数次盒子里面装着什么。他总是告诉我'里面是他最珍视的东西'"。杰克说道。

现在它没了。这所房子中的一切都和杰克的记忆相符，除了那个盒子。他觉得可能是贝尔瑟家的某位亲属把它拿走了。

"而如今我永远也不会知道对贝尔瑟先生来说，他最珍视的是什么了？"杰克说，"妈妈，我最好去睡一会儿。我还要赶明早的飞机回家。"

贝尔瑟先生去世已有两周了。一天杰克下班回家，发现信箱里有一张纸条。

上面写着"邮包需要签字。家里无人。请在三日内到中心邮局

office within the next three days," the note read.

Early the next day Jack retrieved the package.

The small box was old and looked like it had been mailed a hundred years ago. The handwriting was difficult to read, but the return address caught his attention.

"Mr. Harold Belser" it read.

Jack took the box out to his car and ripped open the package. There inside was the gold box and an envelope.

Jack's hands shook as he read the note inside.

"Upon my death, please forward this box and its contents to Jack Bennett. It's the thing I valued most in my life." A small key was taped to the letter.

His heart racing, as tears filling his eyes, Jack carefully unlocked the box. There inside he found a beautiful gold pocket watch. Running his fingers slowly over the finely etched casing, he unlatched the cover.

Inside he found these words engraved: "Jack, Thanks for your time! Harold Belser."

"The thing he valued most...was...my

办理。"

第二天一早，杰克就取回了包裹。

这个小包装箱很旧，看起来好像是一百年以前寄出的。笔迹很难辨认，但是回信地址引起了他的注意。

上面写着"哈罗德·贝尔瑟先生"。

杰克把包装箱拿到车里，撕开包裹。里面装着那个金色的盒子和一个信封。

杰克读着里面的便笺，双手在不停地颤抖。

"我死后，请把这个盒子以及里面的东西转寄给杰克·本尼特。这是我一生中最珍视的东西。"一把小钥匙被胶带粘在信上。

杰克的心狂跳不已，热泪盈眶，他小心翼翼地打开那个盒子。在里面发现了一块漂亮的金色怀表。手指慢慢划过雕刻精美的外壳，他打开了护盖。

他发现里面镌刻着一些字："杰克，谢谢你陪我度过的美好时光！哈罗德·贝尔瑟。"

"他最珍视的东西竟然是……

time."	我陪他度过的时光。"
Jack held the watch for a few minutes, then called his office and cleared his appointments for the next two days.	拿着手表待了片刻,杰克打电话给办公室,取消了未来两天的所有工作预约。
"Why?" Janet, his assistant asked.	"为什么呢?"他的助理珍妮特不解地问。
"I need some time to spend with my son," he said.	"我需要一些时间去陪伴我的儿子。"杰克答道。
"Oh, by the way, Janet...thanks for your time!"	"噢,顺便提一下,珍妮特,谢谢你与我共度的时光。"

Unit Nine

Part I Vocabulary & Structure

Section A

Directions: *In this section, there are 10 incomplete sentences. You are required to complete each one by deciding on the most appropriate word or words from the 4 choices marked A, B, C and D. Then you should mark the corresponding letter on the Answer Sheet with a single line through the center.*

1. I _____ in touch with you as soon as I receive more details from the manager.
    A. am   B. was   C. will be   D. have been
2. Travelling across the country costs a lot of money, but John can _____ it.
    A. spend   B. give   C. build   D. afford
3. It was not until 3:00 p.m. _____ the secretary found the missing report.
    A. where   B. that   C. as   D. while
4. The police have not _____ the search even if it has lasted for a week.
    A. given up   B. taken away C. broken in   D. brought about
5. I decided to _____ as a waiter in a restaurant during my summer vacation.
    A. serve   B. turn   C. take   D. make
6. I'm afraid we don't have that book in stock, _____ we can order it for you.
    A. as   B. but   C. since   D. for
7. In this museum a guided tour _____ for you at no charge.
    A. being provided   B. to provide
    C. is provided   D. provides
8. Generally speaking, a lot of patience is _____ to look after a sick patient.
    A. regarded   B. decided   C. agree   D. required
9. Hold the money in your bank account _____ you use it for college courses.
    A. although   B. as if   C. unless   D. wherever
10. _____ the price of the product, you will have to pay for shipping.
    A. In terms of   B. In addition to
    C. In relation to   D. In spite of

Section B

Directions: *There are 5 incomplete statements here. You should fill in each blank with the proper form of the word given in brackets. Write the word or words in the corresponding space on the Answer Sheet.*

11. The factory is going to make a new model of bicycle, designed (special) _____ for women.

12. It is no use (try) _____ to advertise so much if you don't know the users' need.

13. We are informed that the company meeting will (hold) _____ next Saturday afternoon.

14. You should remember (lock) _____ the door when you leave the office.

15. There is no (possible) _____ for us to get the products before the Spring Festival.

Part II Reading Comprehension

Task 1

Directions: *Read the following passage and make the correct choice.*

Being a salesman, the most important thing is to understand people. You've got to know what they're thinking. If you can figure that out, you can get them to do a lot. They come in with an idea about what they want. You get them talking about themselves, about what they like.

If it's a man, you talk about football, or something like that. If it's a woman, you ask her about fashions. That way they get comfortable with you. You ask them a lot of questions and get them saying yes. Then they just get into the habit of saying yes.

In the end, you can put them into anything you want, if you're really good. For example, if they need a little car for the city, you send them home a truck. Of course, I wouldn't really do that. It wouldn't be right. You've got to sell on this job, but you also have to be fair. It's not fair to take advantage of people too much. There are some people in this business who'd do anything. But I don't believe in that.

1. To be a good salesman, the most important thing is to _____.

    A. learn from different kinds of people

    B. understand what people are thinking

    C. see what people usually do in daily life

    D. watch what changes people have made

2. According to the passage, you can make a woman feel comfortable by _____.
   A. talking about fashions   B. playing football together
   C. sending a small gift to her   D. saying yes to her questions
3. One way to make people get into the habit of saying yes is to _____.
   A. ask them to say what they like
   B. tell them to do anything you want
   C. help them feel confident in themselves
   D. get them to say yes to a lot of your questions
4. According to the last paragraph, the author believes that _____.
   A. it is right to do anything in business
   B. it is useless to believe in what customers say
   C. it is unfair to take too much advantage of people
   D. it is dangerous to listen to the advice of a salesman
5. Which of the following statements is TRUE according to the passage?
   A. Most women like to talk about sports events.
   B. Some business people would do anything to sell.
   C. It's difficult to understand other people very well.
   D. You can make people do anything by talking with them.

Task 2

Directions: *Read the following passage and make the correct choice.*

Computer Care Plan

2-year Service Protection for Desktop Computers

Service you can rely on

We're here when you need us, weekends or weekdays, if any trouble should happen. All it takes is a quick phone call to 877-968-6391 or a visit to our online service center.

Did you know? Most manufacturers' guarantee only covers repairs due to faults in materials. Our computer Care Plan offers so much more!

Terms & Conditions inside

Put in your receipt here. It is needed to register the plan for using the Computer Care Center tools.

Protect what's yours

We protect more than just your computers; we protect your valuable data. Keep your photos, music, e-mail, and financial records safe with the enclosed Computer Care

Center CD.

Rest easy, we have it covered!

No out-of-pocket expenses for covered repairs.

In-home service for desktop computers.

If your product requires three repairs for the same fault, we'll replace it.

Round-the-clock customer service

The Computer Care Center provides an entire year of protection to help keep your family safe and your computer healthy.

Prices

Product	Service Plan
Desktops (under $400)	$49.88
Desktops ($400 and above)	$69.88

6. If there is any trouble with your computer, you can _____.
    A. contact the manufacturer in person
    B. write a letter to the service center
    C. refer to the instructions provided
    D. visit the service center online

7. Most manufacturers' guarantee just covers the repairs of your computer due to _____.
    A. hardware damage   B. wrong operation
    C. material faults   D. missing plan

8. When registering for the use of the Care Center tools, you need to show _____.
    A. the manufacturer's guarantee card
    B. your receipt of the computer
    C. a telephone message record
    D. your credit card number

9. The enclosed Computer Care Center CD is used to _____.
    A. protect your data   B. write your e-mails
    C. take photos   D. play music

10. The product will be replaced if _____.
    A. your valuable data has been lost
    B. you have paid the extra service fee
    C. the same fault needs a third repair
    D. it is within guarantee period

Task 3

Directions: *Read the following passage. After reading it, you should complete the information by filling in the blanks marked 11 to15（**in no more than 3 words**）in the table below. You should write your answers on the Answer Sheet correspondingly.*

  Business memo is frequently used in companies. It is called an intra-company communication because it is used by people in their own company. They change to letters, however, when they write messages to people who do not work for their company.

  A memo creates a written record that may or may not be filed, depending on the receiver and the subject. As you know, spoken language may be misunderstood or forgotten. So, the memo becomes a record that does much to ensure the complete communication between the receiver and the sender.

  The standard form of a memo frequently carries a pre-printed series of items: To, From, Date and Subject. The first two items include the names of the receiver and the sender. A well-written subject line tells the reader the key topic or topics the memo is about.

Business Memo

Range of application: frequently used in ___11___.
Functions: creates a written ___12___ that may not be filed to ___13___ the complete
     communication between the receiver and the sender.
The standard form of a memo includes:
   1) To; 2)___14___; 3) Date; 4)___15___.

Task 4

Directions: *The following is a list of terms of sports. After reading it, you are required to find the items equivalent to those given in chinese in the table below. Then you should mark the corresponding letters in order of the numbered blanks, 16 through 20 on the Answer Sheet.*

A—Track and Field   J—Road Race
B—Cheerleader   K—Platform Diving
C—No. 1 Seed   L—Marathon
D—Chief Referee   M—Figure Skating
E—Long Jump   N—Water-skiing

F—Hammer Throw
G—Semifinal
H—Balance Beam
I—Handball Field
O—Extreme Sports
P—Underwater Swimming
Q—Ice Hockey

Example: （A）田径运动 　　　　（F）链球
16.（　）半决赛 　　　　　　（　）平衡木
17.（　）啦啦队队长 　　　　（　）马拉松
18.（　）花样滑冰 　　　　　（　）手球场
19.（　）跳台跳水 　　　　　（　）潜泳
20.（　）冰球 　　　　　　　（　）跳远

Task 5

Directions: *Read the following passage. After reading it, you are required to complete the answers that follow the questions. You should write your answers **in no more than 3 words***.

Underground tickets are available at all underground stations. Ticket prices for the underground vary according to the distance you travel. The network is divided into five zones: a central zone and four outer zones. Generally, the more zones you travel through, the higher your fare will be. You must buy your ticket before you start your journey, from a ticket office or machine. Keep your ticket for inspection and collection at your destination.

The easiest and most economical way to travel around London is with a travel card. This gives you the freedom of London's trains, tubes, and buses in whichever zones you choose. It's perfect for visitors because one ticket combines travel on the trains of Network Southeast with the underground, Dockland Light railway and most of London buses. It's more convenient than buying separate tickets for each journey. Travel cards are available from any train or tube station.

Travel card season tickets include seven-day, monthly and annual tickets. This is the modern, convenient and flexible ticket for your journey. For travel card season tickets, please bring a passport-size photograph with you.

21. How do the underground ticket prices change?
　　They change according to ＿＿＿＿＿＿＿.
22. Where will the underground tickets be collected?
　　They will be collected ＿＿＿＿＿＿＿.
23. What is the easiest and most economical way to travel around London?
　　It is with ＿＿＿＿＿＿＿.

24. Where can you buy travel cards?

They can be bought from train or _____.

25. What should you take if you want to have a travel card season ticket?

You should take a _____ with you.

Part Ⅲ Translation (English into Chinese)

1. According to a recent survey, there is demand for medical assistants in different areas of medicine.

    A. 各地区统计报告表明，许多地方的医院都急需补充医疗设备。

    B. 调查清楚表明，在许多不同的医疗领域，都需要有医药助理。

    C. 根据最近的一项调查，不同的医学领域对医辅人员都有需求。

2. The road department apologized for any inconvenience caused while road improvements were in progress.

    A. 道路部门对道路改造期间所带来的不便表示歉意。

    B. 道路部门为修建道路可能引起的不便进行了解释。

    C. 道路部门辩解说，新近造成的麻烦是因道路正在改建。

3. Thanks to modern medicine and higher living standards, people live longer now.

    A. 感谢现代医药和生活水平提高，人们长寿了。

    B. 感谢现代医药和生活水平提高，人们现在却不长寿了。

    C. 由于现代医药和生活水平提高，人们现在寿命更长了。

4. The doctor advised Mary to stay in hospital until she was fully recovered.

    A. 医生建议马丽完全康复后再出院。

    B. 医生建议马丽留在医院直到被充分恢复。

    C. 医生建议马丽留在医院不到被充分恢复。

5. Come and join in our walking group. In the 11 week activities, we will help you to improve your health. Each week we will have a class or a walk that will teach you about living a healthier life. We will have a guided shopping tour and fun guided walks. In addition, each member will receive some paper materials about walking.

_____

_____

_____

_____

_____

Part IV Practical Writing

Directions: *This part is to test your ability to do practical writing. You are required to write an e-mail according to the information given below in Chinese. Remember to do your writing on the Translation/Composition Sheet.*

假如你是李峰，和朋友凯特约好本周日去看电影，但你突然有事去不了了。请根据以下要点写一封电子邮件。

日期：2011年4月10日
内容：
1）这周末不能去，表示歉意；
2）解释原因：奶奶突然生病了，需要照顾；
3）建议另约时间在下周末，并为失约表示歉意。

Supplementary Reading

Passage A

First Priority 绝对优先权

A wealthy man and his son loved collecting rare works of art. They had everything in their collection, from Picasso to Raphael.	一个富翁和他的儿子都喜欢收藏珍贵的艺术品。他们的藏品非常丰富，从毕加索到拉斐尔。
Then the son went to war and died in battle. The father grieved deeply for his	后来儿子当了兵，在一场战争中牺牲了。富翁因失去唯一的儿子

only son. Later, he was given a portrait of his son, and though it was a rather ordinary painting, it became very precious to him. When visitors came to the father's home, he would take them to see his son's portrait first, before viewing any of the other great works from his collection.

A few months later, the man died, and there was to be a great auction of his paintings. Many influential people gathered, excited over seeing the great paintings and having an opportunity to purchase one for their very own collection. On the platform sat the painting of the son.

The auctioneer began the auction by announcing, "We will start the bidding with this picture of the son. Who will bid for this picture?" There was silence. Not one person was interested in buying that portrait; they all were intending to buy the more famous paintings.

The auctioneer persisted, "Will someone bid for this painting? Who will start the bidding? $100, $200? What will you give me for the son?"

Finally, the long-time gardener of the man and his son, spoke and said, " I'll give $10 for it, but that's all I can afford."

The auctioneer tried to carry on with the bidding, but by this time the crowd was getting impatient. Somebody angrily called out, "Give it to the gardener for $10. Let's

而伤心欲绝。后来他得到一幅儿子的画像。虽然这是一幅非常普通的画，但对富翁来说，他却视若珍宝。每当有客人造访时，富翁总是带他们先去欣赏儿子的画像，然后再带他们观赏他收藏的名画珍品。

几个月后，富翁去世了。他的名画收藏将被拍卖。许多名人都蜂拥而至，争睹名画的真容同时也想有机会拍得一件珍品为自己的收藏增色。拍卖台上摆放着富翁儿子的画像。

拍卖开始。拍卖师大声宣布："现在首先开始竞拍富翁儿子的画像。谁要竞拍这幅画像？"全场一片静寂，无人应答。没有人想买这幅普通的画像。他们都想买名画。

拍卖师继续喊道："有人竞买这幅画像吗？谁先出价？100 美元，200 美元？有人买吗？你们想出价多少？"

最后，一直在富翁家工作的园丁高声喊道："我出价 10 美元，但那是我倾囊而出了。"

拍卖师继续卖力地推销这幅画像，但是此时焦急等待的人们已开始变得不耐烦。有人愤怒地大喊，"把这张画像以 10 美元的价格卖给

see the master-paintings now. We want more valuable investments for our collections."

"All right then," the auctioneer replied, "Going once, twice, sold for $10!" He then went on to announce "Ladies and Gentlemen, I'm sorry, but the auction is now over."

Immediately, there were surprised expressions and questions asking, "But what about the other paintings?"

The auctioneer apologized, but explained, that the instructions in the will stated clearly, that only the painting of the son would be auctioned. Whoever bought that paintings, would inherit the entire estate, including all the paintings.

Therefore, the man, who took the son, got everything.

Passage B

Lost Arts　遗失的生活艺术

I used to write a lot of letters. I enjoyed taking the time to sit down and think about what to say to a friend far away, what kinds of details to include, what kinds of personal thoughts to share with someone who knew me and liked me enough to keep in touch with me. And even more than writing the letters, I liked receiving them. I liked seeing the envelope, the way that it was sealed and full of mystery. And I liked learning about my friends' lives—what was happening to them, what they were thinking about recently, how they were doing, what kinds of obstacles they were facing and overcoming.

　　Quite simply, though, I don't get letters anymore. I don't know anyone anymore who likes to write letters. I do get e-mails, and from some people I get a lot of them, but the emails simply aren't the same as letters used to be. They tend to be shorter, more to the point, and more information-based. They often don't even have a salutation, and people don't even sign them sometimes—I get just a message as if the person behind the message just doesn't matter somehow.

　　I have to admit that part of the reason I don't write letters any more is because people stopped answering them—I don't want to take the time and make the effort if there's going to be no return on that effort. But perhaps letters should be like love should be—unconditional, sent with no strings (such as expectations of return) attached.

　　I do know that letters were valuable to me in a lot of ways. In writing down the messages, I was forced to think more deeply about the subjects about which I was writing. I had to think of ways to say precisely what I meant, and that often meant clarifying just what I did mean. They forced me to think of what was going on in my

封被封好，而且充满神秘感的样子。我喜欢了解朋友们的生活状况——比如他们正经历着什么样的事情，他们最近在想些什么，他们的生活过得怎样，他们正面临并正在克服哪些障碍等。

　　不过，我现在却再也收不到来信了。我不知道现在还有谁愿意提起笔来写信。现在收到的都是电子邮件，而且有些人还发很多电子邮件给我。然而电子邮件与以往手写的信件完全不同。邮件的内容往往要短一些、更为切题而且信息性更强。发件人甚至省略称呼语，有时人们甚至都不署名——我收到的只是一条信息，好像发信人是谁这一点并不重要。

　　我必须承认，我之所以不再写信，一部分原因是人们不再给我回信——如果我的努力注定得不到任何回复，那我也不愿意花费时间和精力去这么做。但是，或许书信就应该像爱情一样——寄出时不附加任何条件（诸如期盼回信之类）。

　　我很清楚，书信对我来说具有多方面的价值。在写下信息的同时，我不得不对笔下的主题进行更深入的思考。我必须设法精确地表达出我的意思，这就常常意味着要清楚地阐明我的真实想法。书信迫使我回想起生活中所经历的一切。有时若不是因为写信，恐怕我早已将一

life, sometimes helping me to remind myself of some very positive things that might have slipped my mind. They helped me to feel in touch with friends and family.

But now, letter writing seems to be a thing of the past, a lost art. People used to share with each other beautiful letters that shared their hearts and souls and inner passions. But nowadays, it's become rare to get a birthday card in the mail, even.

And there are other lost arts. I used to bake a lot, but now I don't have the time or the audience, and I certainly don't want to eat all that I bake myself. Spending the time preparing the batter, making sure that each ingredient was included in just the right measurements, was almost a meditative activity for me, and I loved going through the process. And I loved even more eating the results. But this art, too, has moved into my past except for on rare occasions.

And speaking of meditative activities, I also used to like to wash dishes by hand. Focusing all my attention on the dishes and the soapy water helped me to center myself, to let the stress of the day leave me as I paid attention to the simple task at hand. I still wash dishes, but not every day as I used to. Some days, the dishwasher is simply too convenient.

It seems that most of the lost arts have to do with a loss of time to be able to

些有意义的事情抛至脑后了。有了书信，我觉得自己可以随时与亲朋好友沟通联络，书信还将我的注意力集中在了这些有意义的事情上，而这也正是我想与他人一同分享的。

但现在看来，写信似乎已经是过去的事了，成为一种遗失的艺术。人们过去常常通过美好的书信，分享彼此的心灵与激情。但如今，就连邮寄的生日贺卡都已经很少收到了。

还有其他一些被遗弃的艺术。我过去经常自己烘烤食品。不过现在我却没有时间再做，也无人来欣赏我的手艺了。我当然不想独自吃完自己烘烤的美食。对我来说，花时间调制面糊，将各种原料按一定量一样不落地调配在一起，几乎是一项颇费脑筋的活动。我也很喜欢这个过程，我更喜欢品尝最终的成果。但如今，除了极少数时候，这一艺术于我而言已成过去。

谈到沉思式的活动，我过去常喜欢用手洗碗。当我专注于手头这项简单的工作时，我全部的注意力都集中到了那些碗碟和满是洁净液的水中，这可以帮我消除一整天的压力。现在我仍然洗碗，但已不像过去那样每天都洗。有时，洗碗机真的很方便。

似乎大多数遗失的艺术都与人们无暇参与其中时间有关，才渐渐

partake in them. Model building, putting puzzles together, going for drives in the country, gardening, even reading books—many of these things are no longer part of our lives because we simply don't have the time for them any more.

But I do miss the lost arts. Let's make some time. Let's carve some time out of our busyness to allow ourselves to do something fun, something that we enjoy a great deal. After all, on the day we die, nobody's going to reward us for the time we spent at or on work, and nobody's going to punish us for time we spent enjoying ourselves and doing things that make us feel fulfilled.

远离了我们的生活。诸如建模、拼图、驾车去乡下兜风、园艺，乃至读书——很多此类活动都已从我们的生活中消失，因为我们实在是没有时间参与这些活动了。

但是我的确想念那些遗失的艺术。让我们抽出一些时间，让我们从忙碌的工作中挤出一些时间来做些有趣的并且深感乐在其中的事情吧。毕竟，当我们离开人世时，没有人会因为我们把时间投入到工作中而奖赏我们，也没有人会因为我们花时间享受生活、充实自我而惩罚我们。

Unit Ten

Part I Vocabulary & Structure

Section A

Directions: *In this section, there are 10 incomplete sentences. You are required to complete each one by deciding on the most appropriate word or words from the 4 choices marked A, B, C and D. Then you should mark the corresponding letter on the Answer Sheet with a single line through the center.*

1. Think over our proposal and let me know whether you agree _____ it.
   A. for   B. in   C. with   D. at

2. Could you please _____ why you can't come to attend the meeting?
   A. explain   B. understand C. give   D. reach

3. It is a fact _____ most deaths from lung cancer are caused by smoking.
   A. that   B. how   C. what   D. which

4. The manager's reply _____ that he was not really interested in the project.
   A. offered   B. showed   C. advised   D. described

5. She didn't tell the reason _____ she was absent from the important lecture.
   A. what   B. which   C. how   D. why

6. It was once a difficult time, but in the end everything, _____ all right.
   A. turned out   B. put up   C. carried away D. gave in

7. You can fly to London this evening _____ you don't mind changing the flight in Paris.
   A. until   B. if   C. where   D. before

8. Food, clothing and shelter are the _____ needs for all of us.
   A. careful   B. attractive C. strange   D. basic

9. I feel it is my responsibility _____ you of our decision.
   A. inform   B. to inform   C. informing   D. informed

10. The staff member were asked to arrive a few minutes earlier before the meeting _____.
    A. will start   B. starts   C. started   D. would start

Section B

Directions: *There are 5 incomplete statements here. You should fill in each blank with the proper form of the word given in brackets. Write the word or words in the corresponding space on the Answer Sheet.*

11. They are now looking for a new way of (treat) _____ the rare disease.

12. I was (deep) _____ moved by what my boss had done for me.

13. If you want to achieve your goals, you have to work (hard) _____ than ever before.

14. Our company has bought two pieces of (equip) _____ for the lab.

15. Up till now, he (work) _____ on software design for 10 years.

Part II   Reading Comprehension

Task 1

Directions: *Read the following passage and make the correct choice.*

So, you love the Internet. It's a great place to find information or go shopping. It's fun, but do you spend a lot of time online? Experts say 6% of Internet users are Internet addicts—they are always online. "Internet addicts are often young people," says one expert, "and they usually have problem with family, friends, work and school."

Go through the following check list. If you answer yes to all these questions, maybe you are an Internet addict.

1. Do you spend a lot of time on the Internet?   ☐ Yes   ☐ No
2. Do you think or talk about the Internet all the time? ☐ Yes   ☐ No
3. Are all your friends "Internet friends"?   ☐ Yes   ☐ No
4. Is the Internet your only hobby?   ☐ Yes   ☐ No
5. Do you ever miss appointments because you are online? ☐ Yes   ☐ No

So, what do you do if you think you are an addict? Go to an advice service. Where is it? On the internet, of course!

1. According to the first paragraph, people find the Internet a great place to _____.

    A. become addicted   B. get information

    C. make money   D. do office work

2. Those who are always online are called _____.

    A. Internet users   B. Internet experts

  C. Internet addicts   D. Internet providers

 3. According to one expert, Internet addicts are often young people who usually _____.

  A. enjoy a lot of hobbies

  B. suffer from poor health

  C. have problems with life and work

  D. take thorough medical examinations

 4. If you want to find out whether you are an Internet addict, you are advised to _____.

  A. go through the check list provided

  B. take a special training course

  C. ask a friend about it

  D. go to see a doctor

 5. This passage is mainly about _____.

  A. the use of the Internet   B. the types of Internet addicts

  C. the advantages of the Internet   D. the signs of an Internet addict

Task 2

Directions: *Read the following passage and make the correct choice.*

Things you should know about your library card

Library Cards

- Cards are free to all library users.
- Cards are renewed annually.
- Your library card enables you to register at other public libraries across the city.

Responsibility.

- Users are responsible for returning all materials borrowed on their card by the date due and for any charges on items that are overdue, lost or damaged.
- Please report your lost card immediately. Items borrowed on the card are still your responsibility.
- Charges for lost or damaged materials are based on the cost and include handling fees.

Renewals

- Most items can be renewed twice unless someone has requested them.
- There are no renewals on DVDs, videos, or CD-ROMs.

Fines

- Borrowing is free if materials are returned by the due date. If your materials are returned late, fines are charged.

- 30 cents per day for most adult items
- 10 cents per day for most junior materials
- $1 per day adult DVDs
- 50 cents for junior DVDs

6. According to the passage, the library card can be registered at _____.
   A. the library only in your neighborhood
   B. other public librarians in the city
   C. college libraries only
   D. all online libraries

7. Users are required to pay charges on items that are _____.
   A. due   B. renewed   C. damaged   D. borrowed

8. If you have lost your library card, you _____.
   A. are still responsible for the items borrowed on that card
   B. have only to pay the cost of the items borrowed
   C. cannot get a new card from the same library
   D. don't need to pay the handling fees

9. According to the passage, you can renew most of the items you borrowed _____.
   A. once only   B. three times
   C. twice at most   D. as often as you like

10. If you don't return the materials by the due date you will be _____.
    A. charged one dollar per day   B. requested to return the card
    C. informed by an e-mail   D. charged a fine

Task 3

Directions: *Read the following passage. After reading it, you should complete the information by filling in the blanks marked 11 to 15（**in no more than 3 words**）in the table below. You should write your answers on the Answer Sheet correspondingly.*

Party A: Shanghai International Trade Corporation
Party B: British AAR Bank Group
JV Company: AAR Trade Company
Notes:

　A　Party B entered into a lease agreement with Party A entitled Phase 1A Lease Agreement dated April 11, 2016 for the Leased Property ("Lease").

　B　At the time the Lease was entered into, the JV Company had not yet been established.

C Under the Contract Schedule of the Lease, Party A and Party B agreed that the JV Company would replace Party B as tenant to the Lease, subject to complying with the terms of the Lease in this regard.

D At the date of this Agreement, the JV Company has been established.

E The parties to this Agreement now wish to acknowledge and further confirm that Party B shall assign all its rights and obligations under the Lease to the JV Company, and the Lease shall be updated on the terms of this Agreement.

An Agreement

Party A: Shanghai International Trade Corporation
Party B: British AAR Bank Group
JV Company: ___11___
Dates of the Lease Agreement: ___12___
Establishment of the JV Company: after the Lease was ___13___
Original Tenant: Party B
New Tenant: ___14___
Update of the Lease: on the terms of ___15___

Task 4

Directions: *The following is a list of terms of tourism. After reading it, you are required to find the items equivalent to those given in chinese in the table below. Then you should mark the corresponding letters in order of the numbered blanks, 16 through 20 on the Answer Sheet.*

A—Market Price
B—Check-in Time
C—Price List
D—Reception Desk
E—Reservation Service
F—Luggage Office
G—Flight Schedule
H—Handling Fee
I—Luggage Rack

J—Identity Card
K—Room Service
L—Luggage Label
M—Telephone Directory
N—Special Line
O—Rate of Exchange
P—Bed Clothes
Q—Credit Card

Examples: (B) 入住时间　　　　　　　　(K) 客房服务
16. ( ) 市场价　　　　　　　　　　 ( ) 行李架

17. （　）价目表　　　　　　　（　）手续费
18. （　）预订服务　　　　　　（　）电话簿
19. （　）行李寄存处　　　　　（　）接待处
20. （　）专线　　　　　　　　（　）兑换率

Task 5

Directions: *Read the following passage. After reading it, you are required to complete the answers that follow the questions. You should write your answers* ***in no more than 3 word.***

Writing a Job Application

Your application is the first contact you will have with an employer. The employer will use it to decide if you are suitable for the job and if he would like to give you an interview.

It is very important to prepare your application with great care. Make it look good and make sure all the information is clear and easy to read. It is better printed with the A4 paper.

The application Letter

There are many ways you can write a letter for a job. Remember, your address, phone number and the date must be on the letter.

Contents

- Refer to where and when you saw the job advertised.
- Give enough information about your former job that is similar to this one.
- Give your telephone number in the letter.
- Close your letter by stating how suitable you are for the job.

If starting with Sir/Madam, the letter always ends with Yours faithfully. If starting with a person's name, it always ends with Yours sincerely.

Sign your name and have your name printed underneath.

21. What will the employer do if he is satisfied with your application?

　　He will give you ＿＿＿＿＿.

22. What is required about the information in your application?

　　The information should be clear and ＿＿＿＿＿.

23. What message should your application letter include?

　　It should include your address, ＿＿＿＿＿ and the date.

24. What should contents cover?

　　The contents should cover where and when you saw this advertisement, the telephone number, how you suit this job and your ＿＿＿＿＿ of this job.

25. What should you end with if you start with a person's name?

You should end with _____.

Part Ⅲ Translation (English into Chinese)

1. Not surprisingly, many scientists predict that such changes in the climate will probably result in hotter days.

    A. 毫不奇怪，许多科学家都预计气候的这些变化可能会导致天气变暖。

    B. 许多科学家都认为天气变暖会改变气候，这并不令人怀疑。

    C. 许多科学家认为这样的变化毫无疑问得可能会导致热天更多。

2. It is widely accepted that the cultural industry has been one of the key industries in developed countries.

    A. 发达国家已普遍接受，文化产业应看成一种关键性的事业。

    B. 大家普遍接受，发达国家应把文化事业看成一种关键产业。

    C. 人们普遍认为，文化产业已成为发达国家的一个支柱产业。

3. These programs are important to business success and will also contribute to the community at large.

    A. 这些规划对于商业成功十分重要，并有助于将其成果奉献给社会。

    B. 这些程序的成功与做生意一样重要，并且有益于扩大社区的规模。

    C. 这些项目对商业的成功至关重要，还会在总体上对社区做出贡献。

4. The improvement of energy efficiency in a restaurant will not only save money, but protect valuable natural resources, too.

    A. 提高餐厅的效益不仅能够赚钱，而且能够保持珍贵的自然资源。

    B. 提高餐厅的能源效率不仅能省钱，而且能保护宝贵的自然资源。

    C. 减少餐厅的消费虽然省不了多少钱，但能减少自然资源的浪费。

5. Now people have a choice about where they work and what kind of work they'll do. They are faced with the challenge of deciding where to go. They need to know what standard to use in making their decisions. This book provided them with practical advice for making their choices. Meanwhile, they will know what questions to ask, what jobs to look for, and how to make their final decisions.

Part IV Practical Writing

Directions: *This part is to test your ability to do practical writing. You are required to write a note for leave according to the information given below in Chinese. Remember to do your writing on the Translation/Composition Sheet.*

说明：假如你是王林，因为骑车不小心摔到，导致腿部受伤，需向班主任张老师请三天假。请写一则请假条，内容包括：
1）请假原因；
2）请假日期：4月8—10日；
3）落下的功课会在返校后补上；
4）希望班主任准假。

Words for reference: 骑车摔倒 fall off the bicycle 腿部受伤 hurt one's leg 请假 ask for ...-day leave

Supplementary Reading

Passage A

A Five-finger Discount   顺手牵糖

The Belfast, Maine of my youth was not the coastal tourist village that it is today. At the time, Belfast was still a blue-collar town. McDonald's hadn't yet moved into town. Before the supermarket existed, Cottle's, a food market where my dad worked, was the only place where my mother could do her once-a-week shopping. Because we lived a few miles from Belfast, we'd usually	我小的时候，缅因州的贝尔法斯特还不是如今这样的海滨旅游小镇。那个时候，这座小镇还是一座蓝领小镇。麦当劳还没有进驻。在超市出现前，爸爸工作的科特尔食品商场成了妈妈每周一次购物唯一可去的地方。由于我们住得离贝尔法斯特有几英里远，所以我们常常在购物的时候顺便去看望外

combine the grocery trip with a visit to see my grandmother. Of course, Grammy Stairs always had cookies ready for the grandkids.

On one particular shopping day at Cottle's, I stood behind my mother as she was unloading the grocery cart and checking her items out at the register. The candy displays on either side of me were full of Life Savers, Clark Bars, Tootsie Rolls, Sugar Babies—you name it!

"Can I get some candy?" I asked.

My mother rarely veered from her list so I wasn't surprised with her response "No."

This much I knew for certain. "No" always meant "No." There was no sense in me asking a second time. But I really, really wanted that candy!

I reached for a Sugar Baby package. My mother didn't notice. So I figured she probably wouldn't notice if I ever so coyly stuffed them into my pocket. We continued checking out and walked with the bag boy to the car where he loaded the bags into the car's trunk. No one detected my action—not my mother, not the cashier, not the bag boy—no one! I did it! Wow! My very first shoplifting experience! A five-finger discount! How exciting! How easy! How rewarding! Got my candy and didn't need

婆。当然啦,外婆总是为我们这些小孩子准备好饼干吃。

有一天去科特尔商场购物。妈妈在收银台前从购物车里拿出所买的货品逐项结账,而我就站在她身后。我两旁的货架上摆满了各式各样的糖果——有Life Savers薄荷糖、花生酱夹心巧克力,Clark Bars乳糖、Tootsie Rolls 咀嚼糖,Sugar Babies 牛奶焦饴糖——各种品牌,应有尽有。

"我能买点糖吗?"我问妈妈。

妈妈的注意力几乎全在清单上,因此她回答"不行"的时候我并不意外。

对此我十分肯定。"不行"就意味着"不行"。我再问第二遍毫无意义。但是我真的真的很想吃糖!

我把手伸向一袋 Sugar Baby 糖,妈妈并未注意到我。因此我想,如果我非常小心地把它们塞进衣兜里,妈妈很可能不会发现的。我们继续结账,然后随着打包服务生一起走到车前,服务生把购物袋放进后备厢。谁也没有发现我的偷窃行为——无论是我妈妈、收银员还是打包服务生——没有任何人发现!我成功了!哇!我平生第一次体验商店行窃!一次顺手牵羊!多么令人激动!多么轻而易举!多么

one penny to get it!

I sat in the back seat as my mother drove across the bridge to where my grandmother lived. Slowly, so as not to make any unnecessary crinkling noise, I opened my prize and carefully slipped a Sugar Baby in my mouth. No one piece of candy ever tasted so good! She might have said, "No," but I'd said, "Yes," and look who'd won!

When we pulled into my grandmother's driveway, I knew I was in the clear. Miles and minutes separated me from Cottle's. As I prepared to open my car door, I confidently slipped a few more Sugar Babies into my mouth. They would tide me over until I got to Grammy Stairs' cookie jar inside.

Big mistake. "Keith, what have you got in your mouth?" I looked up at the rearview mirror and could see the reflection of my mother's eyes staring intently back at me. "I asked you a question! What have you got in your mouth?"

Though I'd recently become skilled in the art of shoplifting, I hadn't quite mastered the art of giving false testimony. "Uhhh... just some Sugar Babies."

"Sugar Babies? Where did you get the money to buy them?" Why was she asking such a foolish question? She knew I hadn't purchased them. It was no big deal. Nobody

有收获！我得到了这些糖却无须花费分文！

妈妈驾车通过一座桥，向外婆家驶去，而我则坐在后座上。为了避免发出不必要的声音，我慢慢地打开自己的战利品，然后小心翼翼地把一块 Sugar Baby 糖偷偷塞进了嘴里。再没有比这更好吃的糖啦！妈妈或许说过"不行"但是我却说"行"，看看最终是谁赢了！

当我们驶入通往外婆家的车道时，我认为我安全了——距离和时间使我远离了科特尔商场。我一边准备打开车门，一边安心地把几块 Sugar Babies 糖放进嘴里。它们甜美的味道会一直伴随我进入外婆家直到我拿起饼干罐。

这样做真是大错特错。"基思，你嘴里吃什么东西呢？"我抬头看向后视镜，发现妈妈正从镜子里目不转睛地盯着我。"我问你呢？你嘴里吃什么东西呢？"

虽然我刚刚熟练掌握了入店行窃术，但我却尚不精于提供假证词。"呃……就是一些 Sugar Babies 糖。"

"Sugar Babies 糖？你哪来的钱买糖？"妈妈怎么会问我这样一个愚蠢的问题？她知道我根本就没买过。没什么大不了的。根本就

even saw me take them. It was one little package of Sugar Babies. Let's just go into Grammy's!" "I... uh... didn't really buy them."

"That's what I thought!" And then, rather than just going into Grammy's house and giving me a good scolding, she began backing out of my grandmother's driveway.

As she drove away from my grandmother's house and then back across the bridge, I knew exactly where we were headed. To Cottle's! This was so stupid! We're talking twenty-five cents here! A return trip all the way back there was a ridiculous waste of gas and time, if you asked me. Why was she turning this into such an emotional drama? What was she trying to prove?

I didn't have long to find out.

My mother pulled into Cottle's parking lot, cast one more glare my way, and marched me into the store. She proceeded to hunt down Mr. Proulx, the store manager! Why would she want to bother an important man like Mr. Proulx about me needing to pay for some candy that any cashier could more easily just take care of?

Once she located him and got his full attention, she said, in a voice that could be heard from three aisles away, "Tell Mr. Proulx what you did!"

没人看见我拿糖了。不就是一小袋 Sugar Babies 糖吗？赶紧进外婆家吧！"我……呃……其实我并没买。"

"果然不出我所料！"接着，妈妈既没有进外婆家，也没有狠狠批评我，而是把车倒出了外婆家的车道。

等妈妈将车驶离了外婆家再次穿过那座桥的时候，我清楚地知道我们将前往何处。去科特尔商场！真是太傻了！不过是一袋 25 美分的糖而已！如果你问我，我会说：开车大老远原路返回真够可笑的，既费油又费时。为什么妈妈要小题大做呢？她想要证明什么呢？

没过多久我就找到了答案。

妈妈把车停入科特尔商场的停车场，又瞪了我一眼，带着我走进商场。她立即四处寻找商场经理——普鲁克斯先生。补付糖果钱这样一个收银员都能轻松处理的事情，她何必要麻烦像普鲁克斯先生这样重要的人呢？

一发现普鲁克斯先生且让他把注意力全集中到我们身上时，妈妈就用三个过道以外都能听得见的大嗓门说道，"告诉普鲁克斯先生你的所作所为！"

I knew Mr. Proulx. I liked Mr. Proulx. But on this day Mr. Proulx was taking all of his cues from my mother. There was no room for doubt... I was on trial and Mr. Proulx was judge and jury! Through tears, I admitted what I had done and apologized. My mother put a quarter in my hand to give to him. Mr. Proulx listened and accepted my apology along with the twenty-five cents. He then issued a stern warning, explaining what the consequences would be if there was ever a repeat performance. Snuffling, embarrassed, ashamed, I totally understood the significance of my actions and what they might lead to if not nipped in the bud: Sugar Babies today, grand theft auto tomorrow. To this day, often while in a checkout lane near a candy rack, I think back to the lesson I learned from my mother. Thanks, Mom, for keeping me from a life of crime.	我认识普鲁克斯先生。我喜欢他。但是那天他完全领会了妈妈的意图。毋庸置疑，我在受审，而普鲁克斯先生就是法官和陪审团！我流着眼泪承认了之前所做的一切并道了歉。妈妈把25美分放到我的手里，让我转交给普鲁克斯先生。他听着我的讲述，接受了我的道歉，收下了25美分。然后，他向我提出严厉警告，告诉我如果再犯后果将会如何。我抽噎着，羞愧难当，完全意识到了自己行为的严重性，也知道了如果没有将它扼杀在萌芽中最终会导致什么结果——今天偷糖小贼，明天窃车大盗。 直到今天，当我站在糖果架附近的付款通道里时，我还是会想起妈妈给我上的这一课。谢谢你，妈妈，是你让我远离了犯罪的道路。

Passage B

Egg Drop Soup　　蛋花汤

"OK, everybody. It's that time of year," said my science teacher, Mr. Beal. "This Friday we'll have the annual Egg Drop Challenge." A couple of my classmates groaned, but no one was at all surprised. Mr. Beal's fifth-grade Egg Drop Challenge was an institution at my school. The goal of the Challenge was simple—you had to build a protective container to keep an egg from	"好了，同学们。又到了每年的这个时候，"我的理科老师比尔说道，"本周五我们将举行一年一度的摔蛋挑战赛。" 听完这话，几个同学发出了抱怨声，不过大家一点儿也不感到惊讶。在我们学校，比尔老师组织的五年级摔蛋挑战赛已经成为一项由来已久的赛事。这项挑战赛的目标很简单——你得为一枚鸡蛋制

breaking when dropped over the stadium wall.

"Bring your containers to class on Friday," Mr. Beal said. "By the way, this year we're going to try something different. You can work alone or with a partner."

My best friend, Cassie, and I grinned at each other. We always worked on projects together. She's brainy; I'm creative. We're the perfect combination. Like peanut butter and marshmallow cream.(which happens to be my favorite kind of sandwich.)

I made my favorite sandwich that afternoon while waiting for Cassie to come over and work on the container. Spreading the fluffy marshmallow cream gave me an idea.

"I have a brilliant design for our egg container!" I said when Cassie arrived.

"What?" Cassie asked eagerly.

"We can cushion it with some marshmallow cream."

"Huh?"

"You know, to absorb the shock of the impact," I explained.

"You've got to be kidding, Laura."

作一个容器,以保护鸡蛋从体育场的墙上落下来时不会被摔碎。

"周五把你们做好的容器带到班上来。"比尔老师说,"哦,对了,今年我们将尝试改变一下规则。你们可以自己独立完成,也可以找个搭档合作。"

我和我最要好的朋友卡西相视而笑。我们俩总是一块做各种课题。她博学多才,我创意非凡。我们俩珠联璧合,就像是花生酱与棉花糖霜。(这碰巧是我最爱吃的那种味道的三明治。)

于是那天下午,我一边等着卡西过来和我一起制作容器,一边做着我最爱吃的那种口味的三明治。在往三明治上涂抹松软的棉花糖霜时,我脑袋里蹦出了一个主意。

"我想到了一个绝妙的鸡蛋容器设计!"卡西一到我家,我便对她说道。

"是什么?"卡西急切地问道。

"我们可以用棉花糖霜为它做个衬垫。"

"哈?"

"那个,可以吸收撞击所产生的震动。"我解释着。

"劳拉,你一定是在开玩笑。"

"You have a better idea?"

Cassie pointed to a sketch in her notebook. "Actually, I do. We put the egg in a basket with parachute attached. It will simply float to safety."

"It's too easy for something to go wrong. It will never work!" I said.

"And marshmallow cream will?" Cassie rolled her eyes. "The parachute is better than that stupid idea."

I couldn't believe it. Of course we'd had our little fights in the past, but this was different. She'd never called any of my ideas "stupid" before.

"Oh, yeah?" I said.

"Yeah!"

And just like that, our friendship was smashed.

"Then I'll build mine and you build yours, and we'll just see whose is better."

"Fine!" Cassie shoved her notebook into her backpack and stormed out.

And just like that, our friendship was smashed. Like an egg dropped from the top of a stadium without marshmallow cream to

"你有更好的主意吗?"

卡西指着她笔记本上的一张草图说:"不错,我确实有。我们可以把鸡蛋放进一个系有降落伞的篮子里。这样它便能安全地降落了。"

"这样太容易出错了。绝对行不通!"我说。

"用棉花糖霜就行得通?"卡西冲我翻了翻白眼。"降落伞比那个蠢主意好多了。"

我简直不敢相信自己的耳朵。诚然,过去我们也曾有过一些争吵和摩擦,但是这次却有所不同。以前她从未把我的任何主意称作"蠢主意"。

"哦,是吗?"我说。

"没错!"

就这样,我们的友谊破碎了。

"那好,我做我的,你做你的,等着瞧到底谁的容器更好。"

"很好!"卡西把她的笔记本胡乱塞进书包,怒气冲冲地走了。

就这样,我们的友谊破碎了。仿佛一枚没有棉花糖霜保护的鸡蛋,从体育场顶部坠落下来。

protect it.

When Friday finally rolled around, I had to admit that Cassie's Egg Force One looked pretty good. She had used a handkerchief to create a small parachute. It was tied to a basket that held styrofoam packing peanuts and, in the center of it all, her egg.

My Egg-cellent Egg Cream didn't look quite so scientific. I had lined the sides and bottom of a small box with rice cakes. Then I'd added a layer of marshmallow cream, the egg, and a layer of Jell-O.

This is how the competition worked: All the students in my class carried their egg containers up three stadium steps and dropped them over the side wall. If your egg broke, you were out. If the egg survived, you had to walk up three more steps and drop it again. This went on until the last egg broke.

By the fourth launch, only Cassie and I were left.

"OK," Mr. Beal yelled. "Let'em go on the count of three."

"Good luck, Laura," Cassie said, turning to me. "You're going to need it."

I didn't respond. I figured winning would be sweeter revenge.

终于又到了周五，我不得不承认卡西的"蛋军一号"看起来相当不错。她用一块手帕做了一个小降落伞。降落伞系在篮子上，篮子里装有用泡沫塑料包裹着的花生，在篮子的中心放着她的鸡蛋。

而我的"蛋霜之王"看上去就没那么有科学性。我先用米糕将一个小盒子里的四边和底部垫好。然后铺上一层棉花糖霜，再放入鸡蛋，最后加上一层吉露果冻。

比赛是这样进行的：班里的所有同学拿着自己的鸡蛋容器在体育场里向上走三层台阶，然后让它们从边墙下落下来。如果你的鸡蛋碎了，你就出局了。如果鸡蛋完好无损，你就必须再向上走三层台阶，再次让鸡蛋落下。直到最后一个鸡蛋破碎，比赛才会结束。

比赛进行到第四轮时，只剩下我和卡西了。

"好，"比尔老师高声喊道。"数到三，然后放手。"

"劳拉，祝你好运。"卡西转向我说道。"这回你可得碰运气了。"

我没有回答。我认为赢得胜利将会是更痛快的复仇。

The class called, "One, two, three!" I let go of my box.

"Ew," I heard someone say after a minute. Had my egg broken? I raced down the steps, trying to get to the bottom before Cassie did.

The side walk was already dotted with egg shells from previous failed drops. I finally found my brave little Egg-cellent Egg Cream. I didn't even have to open the box to see the results. Yolk and egg white mixed with yellow Jell-O seeped from the corner.

"That looks like egg drop soup, Laura," Cassie said. She was holding her Egg Force One. My heart raced. Had she won? I looked at her basket. Empty.

"My egg bounced out," she explained, pointing to a broken shell in the grass.

"I guess the pilot had an egg-jector seat," I offered.

Cassie looked at me, and her glare softened. I could see it in the corners of her eyes. She was trying not to smile. I grinned. She giggled.

"Egg-jector seat," she said.

"Egg drop soup," I said, laughing until I had tears in my eyes.

全班同学喊着:"一, 二, 三!"我松开了手中的盒子。

"哎唷。"随即我听到有人发出这种声音。我的鸡蛋碎了吗?我冲下台阶,想赶在卡西之前到达地面。

边墙下的走道已经星星点点地布满了前几轮比赛中摔碎的鸡蛋壳。我终于找到了我那枚小小的勇敢的"蛋霜之王"。我甚至没有必要打开盒子来检查结果。蛋黄和蛋清混合着黄色的果冻从盒角渗了出来。

"劳拉,那看上去像蛋花汤。"卡西说。她正握着她的"蛋军一号"。我的心在狂跳。她赢了吗?我看了看她的篮子。是空的。

"我的鸡蛋弹出去了。"她指着草丛里破碎的蛋壳解释着。

"我猜这位飞行员有把蛋射座椅。"我接着她的话说道。

卡西看着我,我可以从她的眼角看出,她的目光渐渐柔和下来。她想忍住不笑。我咧着嘴笑了。她也咯咯地笑了起来。

"蛋射座椅。"她说。

"蛋花汤。"我边说边笑着,直到泪水充满了双眼。

"A tie," Mr. Beal said, shaking his head.	"平局。"比尔老师摇了摇头说。
But Cassie and I knew we'd won something more important than the Egg Drop Challenge. Some friendships aren't like eggs after all. They can survive a little bouncing.	但我和卡西深知我们赢得了比摔蛋挑战赛更重要的东西。某些友谊绝对不像鸡蛋一样。它们不会因为小矛盾而破碎。

高等学校英语应用能力考试（B级）
2016年12月真题

Part I Listening Comprehension (25 minutes)

Directions: *This part is to test your listening ability. It consists of 4 sections.*

Section A

Directions: *This section is to test your ability to give proper responses. There are 7 recorded questions in it. After each question, there is a pause. The questions will be spoken two times. When you hear a question, you should decide on the correct answer from the 4 choices marked A), B), C) and D) given in your test paper. Then you should mark the corresponding letter on the Answer Sheet with a single line through the center.*

1. A) Sorry, he's not in.   C) Try again, please.
   B) Here you are.   D) Thank you.

2. A) Nice to see you.   C) No, I don't.
   B) See you later.   D) Take care.

3. A) See you next time.   C) You are welcome.
   B) No, thanks.   D) Press the button here.

4. A) Over there.   C) I like Chinese food.
   B) Yes, I do.   D) Tomorrow morning.

5. A) Never mind.   C) Only a week.
   B) Certainly.   D) My pleasure.

6. A) On the Internet.   C) By bus.
   B) She's very nice.   D) It's far away.

7. A) We are busy.   C) It's expensive.
   B) Take it easy.   D) He's very kind.

Section B

Directions: *This section is to test your ability to understand short dialogues. There are 7 recorded dialogues in it. After each dialogue, there is a recorded question. Both the* dialogues and questions will be spoken two times. When you hear a question, you should decide on the correct answer from the 4 choices marked A), B), C) and D) given in your test paper. Then you should mark the corresponding letter on the Answer Sheet with a single line through the center.

8. A) Earth Day. C) Father's Day.
   B) Mother's Day. D) Thanksgiving Day.
9. A) Flight numbers. C) Banking services.
   B) Bus schedules. D) Office hours.
10. A) How to book a flight. C) When to hand in the form.
    B) Where to sign the name. D) Whom to ask for help.
11. A) From newspapers. C) From magazines.
    B) From the sales department. D) From the website.
12. A) The development plan. C) Sales of a new product.
    B) The market share. D) Costs of advertising.
13. A) When to get the orders. C) How to pay for the goods.
    B) Where to obtain the price list. D) Whom to contact.
14. A) It has over 500 employees. C) It has several branches.
    B) It was started in 1998. D) It is located in Beijing.

Section C

Directions: *In this section, there are 2 recorded conversations. After each conversation, there are some recorded questions. Both the conversations and questions will be spoken two times. When you hear a question, you should decide on the correct answer from the 4 choices marked A), B), C) and D) given in your test paper. Then you should mark the corresponding letter on the Answer Sheet with a single line through the center.*

Conversation 1

15. A) Making a sales plan. C) Doing a market survey.
    B) Preparing an annual report. D) Writing a business letter.
16. A) It costs much less. C) Most old people like it.
    B) It saves time. D) Most young people like it.

Conversation 2

17. A) He has got a summer job. C) He has just visited a park.
    B) He has lost his job. D) He has been to the beach.
18. A) A sales person. C) A manager assistant.
    B) A tour guide. D) A computer programmer.
19. A) Because the salary is too low.

B) Because the company is too small.

C) Because she has to travel abroad frequently.

D) Because a tour guide has to work long hours.

Section D

Directions: *In this section you will hear a recorded short passage. The passage is printed in the test paper, but with some words or phrases missing. The passage will be read three times. During the second reading, you are required to put the missing words or phrases on the Answer Sheet in order of the numbered blanks according to what you hear. The third reading is for you to check your writing. Now the passage will begin.*

Good evening, ladies and gentlemen!

First of all, I'd like to __20__ a sincere welcome to you all, the new comers of our company. As you know, our company is one of the top 50 companies in the country and has a history of more than 100 years. I think you must __21__ being a member of such a great company. But we cannot __22__ tradition alone. We need new employees with new knowledge and creative __23__.

I would like to welcome you __24__, and from today, let's begin to work together.

Part II Vocabulary & Structure (10 minutes)

Directions: *This part is to test your ability to construct correct and meaningful sentences. It consists of 2 sections.*

Section A

Directions: *In this section, there are 10 incomplete sentences. You are required to complete each one by deciding on the most appropriate word or words from the 4 choices marked A), B), C) and D). Then you should mark the corresponding letter on the Answer Sheet with a single line through the center.*

25. Their talks next week are expected to focus _____ business management.

    A) on   B) with   C) in   D) of

26. There are no openings at present, so the company will not _____ anybody.

    A) handle   B) lead   C) hire   D) dismiss

27. I wanted to know when and where we should _____ our assignments.

    A) set back   B) fall into   C) take off   D) hand in

28. We considered _____ to California at first, but decided not to in the end.

    A) move   B) moving   C) to move   D) moved

29. Australia has its own _____ identity, which is very different from that of

Britain.

    A) busy   B) central   C) capable   D) cultural

30. The Internet allows rural school children _____ about what is happening in the world.

    A) to learn   B) learning   C) learn   D) learned

31. The grocery store has been closed down since no one wanted to _____ the business.

    A) put up   B) give off   C) take over   D) bring about

32. The CEO said that it would never be _____ late to apologize for its poor service.

    A) much   B) too   C) so   D) very

33. The president gave a detailed _____ of his proposal at the meeting.

    A) explanation   B) search   C) balance   D) word

34. Last year the employees in our department were so busy _____ they were not able to take a vacation.

    A) which   B) what   C) who   D) that

Section B

Directions: *There are 5 incomplete statements here. You should fill in each blank with the proper form of the word given in brackets. Write the word or words in the corresponding space on the Answer Sheet.*

35. (Surprising) _____, the team was able to finish the task two weeks ahead of schedule.

36. The designers from our firm are ready (assist) _____ you throughout the whole process.

37. It seems to me that his solution is much (effective) _____ than mine.

38. Your strong determination to improve services has left a deep (impress) _____ on us.

39. We are pleased to have you visit us and look forward to (meet) _____ you next week.

Part Ⅲ Reading Comprehension (35 minutes)

Directions: *This part is to test your reading ability. There are 5 tasks for you to fulfill. You should read the reading materials carefully and do the tasks as you are instructed.*

Task 1

Directions: *After reading the following passage, you will find 5 questions or unfinished statements, numbered 40 to 44. For each question or statement, there are 4 choices marked A), B), C) and D). You should mark the correct choice and mark the corresponding letter on the Answer Sheet with a single line through the center.*

What Can E-medical (E-med) Offer?

We offer advices with your own private online doctor by e-mail or phone. If we cannot sort out your problems in that manner, we can refer you to a specialist (专家) in the field you need for further investigations or examination.

What if you cannot make a diagnosis (诊断) by e-mail?

When we receive your e-mail and the doctor feels that he needs to speak to you to discuss your problems, he will call you immediately and we can help you that way.

But if we feel it is necessary, we may ask you to have a video consultation to make a diagnosis or to treat you, or even refer you to a specialist.

What about medical investigations?

If you need further medical investigations to work towards a diagnosis, such as blood tests or scans (扫描), your e-med doctor can usually refer you to a hospital in London. Other medical investigations can also be arranged remotely. The result will be sent to your e-med doctor, who can then advise you on what to do next.

40. We can learn from the passage that e-med service provides medical advices _____.
    A) through a doctor's visit
    B) at a community hospital
    C) from a medical center
    D) by e-mail or phone

41. If e-med service is unable to find out your problem, you will be _____.
    A) sent to a community hospital
    B) asked to wait for a solution
    C) referred to a specialist
    D) given further advices

42. If necessary, the e-med doctor will ask you to _____.
    A) pay him a personal call
    B) have a video consultation
    C) have an immediate operation
    D) pay for the service in advance

43. The e-med doctors will refer the patients to a hospital in London if _____.
    A) medical investigations cannot be arranged
    B) they think that further diagnosis is needed
    C) patients insist on being sent to the hospital
    D) patients are not satisfied with the diagnosis

44. Which of the following can be used as a title of the passage?

A) E-medical Service
B) Video Medical Consultation
C) Traditional Medical Diagnosis
D) Remote Medical Investigation

Task 2

Directions: *The following is a poster. After reading it, you will find 3 questions or unfinished statements, numbered 45 to 47. For each question or statement, there are 4 choices marked A), B), C) and D). You should make the correct choice and mark the corresponding letter on the Answer Sheet with a single line through the center.*

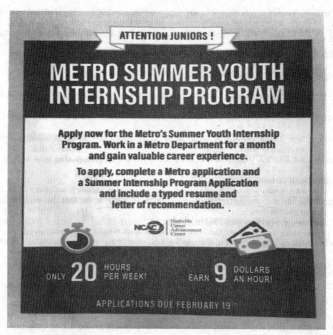

Notes: internship 实习   recommendation 推荐

45. What is advertised in the poster?
    A) A language training program.   C) A summer camp program.
    B) A youth internship program.   D) A volunteer program.

46. By joining the program, the applicants will _____.
    A) improve communication skills   C) gain career experience
    B) obtain a chance to go abroad   D) get a diploma

47. How many hours will the applicants work each week?
    A) 16 hours.   B) 18 hours.   C) 20 hours.   D) 24 hours.

Task 3

Directions: *Read the following letter. After reading it, you should complete the information by filling in the blanks marked 48 to 52 (**in no more than 3 words**) in the* table below. You should write your answers on the Answer Sheet correspondingly.

December 9, 2016

Dear Committee Members and Guests:

　　Welcome to the Energy Capital of the World—Houston, Texas! You are warmly invited to attend the Spring 2017 Meeting of the IEEE/PES Transformers Committee (变压器协会), to be held on March 7–11,2017. It is the sincere pleasure of Tulstar Products, Inc. to be your host for the event.

　　The meeting will be held at the Omni Houston Hotel, located at Four Riverway, Houston, Texas (www.omnihouston.com). The hotel is located on the west side of Houston, in the Uptown Post Oak area, about 10 minutes from downtown. The group rate for guest rooms in the Omni Houston Hotel is US $139 per night(single or double rooms), with rooms reserved under the group name "IEEE Transformers". Please contact the hotel directly for room reservations +713-871-8181 and mention our group name.

　　　　　The Institute of Electrical and Electronics Engineers, Inc.(IEEE)
　　　　　　　　　　www.transformerscommittee.org

Invitation Letter

Date: December 9, 2016

To: __48__ and guests

From: The Institute of Electrical and Electronics Engineers, Inc.(IEEE)

The meeting

Name: Spring 2017 Meeting of the IEEE/PES Transformers Committee

Time: __49__, 2017

Host: Tulstar Products, Inc.

Location: __50__ Hotel

Address: Four Riverway, Houston, Texas

Group room reservation

Group rate for guest rooms: __51__ per night

Group name: __52__

Contact telephone: +713-871-8181

Task 4

Directions: *The following is a list of terms used in the advertising industry. After reading it, you are required to find the item equivalent to those given in Chinese in the table below. Then you should mark the corresponding letters in order of the numbered*

blanks, 53 through 57, on the Answer Sheet.

A—Advertising Budget
B—Advertising Cost
C—Art Direct
D—Brand Loyalty
E—Brand Manager
F—Click Rate
G—Commercial Advertising
H—Consumer Behavior
I—Customer Relation Management
J—Digital Marketing
K—Direct Mail
L—Interactive Advertising
M—Advertising Manager
N—Local Advertising
O—Page View
P—Senior Copy Write
Q—Target Audience

Examples: (J) 数字营销	(P) 资深文案
53. (　) 广告部经理	(　) 品牌忠诚度
54. (　) 目标受众	(　) 消费者行为
55. (　) 广告预算	(　) 直接邮寄
56. (　) 艺术指导	(　) 客户关系管理
57. (　) 品牌经理	(　) 点击率

Task 5

Directions: *Read the following letter. After reading it, you are required to complete the answers that follow the questions (No.58 to No.62). You should write your answers (**in no more than 3 words**) on the Answer Sheet correspondingly.*

Dear Sir,

　　I recently purchased a computer from your store. When I got home, the computer was unable to connect to any network. So I installed the latest operating system on it and that still did not fix the problem.

　　I attempted to return it to your store. However, your staff refused to accept the return because it had the operating system installed on it. But no return policy can be found on the receipt, nor has anyone informed me that I cannot return the computer if I have installed an operating system.

　　Additionally, your staff at this store was very rude when refusing the return and refused to let me speak to the store manager.

　　I request you accept the return or refund the money back to me. A copy of the receipt is attached (including your stated terms and conditions for a return).

Sincerely,
Tony Brown

58. What problem did the writer find with the computer when he got it back home?

　　It was unable to connect to _____.

59. What did the writer do to fix the computer's problem?

　　He installed the latest _____.

60. Why does the writer think he has the right to return the computer?

　　Because no such return policy can be found _____.

61. What did the writer complain about the staff?

　　They were _____.

62. What is attached to the letter?

　　A _____ of the receipt.

Part Ⅳ　Translation—English into Chinese (25 minutes)

Directions: *This part, numbered 63 to 67, is to test your ability to translate English into Chinese. Each of the four sentences (No.63 to No.66) is followed by three choices of suggested translation marked A), B) and C). Make the best choice and write the corresponding letter on the Answer Sheet with a single line through the center. And then write your translation of the paragraph* (No.67) in *the corresponding space on the Translation/Composition Sheet.*

63. To serve our club members better, we continually seek opportunities to open more clubs around the world.

　　A) 为了提高俱乐部成员的整体素养，我们一直以各种不同的方式为大家提供免费的培训。

　　B) 为了更好地为我们俱乐部会员服务，我们不断寻找机会在世界各地开设更多的俱乐部。

　　C) 为了使我们俱乐部的成员享受更好的服务，我们继续寻求机会与世界各地的俱乐部合作。

64. Changing jobs frequently gives you a lot of different experiences in different environments, which shows you can adapt quickly.

　　A) 频繁更换工作使你在不同环境下具有众多的经验，这就表明你能很快地适应。

　　B) 不同的工作让你学会更快地适应环境，积累的不同经验也会带给你更多机遇。

　　C) 经常换工作让你体验在不同环境中的许多工作感受，从而学会迅速适应环境。

65. I am grateful for all the arrangement for this visit, and I enjoyed everything

of it.

A) 我对你们的这次安排深表谢意，你们组织的所有活动我都参加。
B) 这次访问我们收获颇丰，我学到了你们的丰富经验，印象深刻。
C) 非常感谢你们对这次访问的所有安排，每一项安排我都很满意。

66. If you include a photo in your application while not asked for, an employer can assume you rely on your looks.

A) 求职信通常需要附一张照片，老板会因为看到过你的照片而对你产生印象。
B) 虽然未要求在求职函中附一张照片，但你还是附了照片，老板就会认为你可靠。
C) 虽没要求，如果你还是在求职信中附了照片，雇主会认为你想靠颜值取胜。

67. The road construction will start on Monday, January 9th, 2017. It is expected to last one month. The area between 7th Street and 9th Street will be completely closed.

We apologize for any inconvenience this may cause you but the construction work is to make the roads safer. Thank you for your understanding.

If you have any questions regarding the construction, please call at (650) 903-6311.

Part V　Writing (25 minutes)

Directions: *This part is to test your ability to do practical writing. You are required to complete an application form according to the following information given in Chinese. Remember to do your writing on the Translation/Composition Sheet.*

说明：假定你是人力资源部的员工李建新，请根据下列内容填写一份加班申请表。

申请日期：2017年3月1日

部门：人力资源部（Human Resources Department）

加班时间：2017年3月5日 9:00 a.m.—5:00 p.m.

总加班时间：不超过八小时

加班原因：公司最近需要招聘各类员工。人力资源部一周前登了招聘广告，并已收到很多求职信（application letter）。为了协助各部门安排面试，本人需要在周六加班一天，了解应聘人员情况，并安排面试。

Request Date:　　(1)　　

Employee's Name:　　(2)　　

Department:　　(3)

Date of Overtime: March 5, 2017
Overtime Needed: From _____(4)_____ to 5:00 p.m.
Total Overtime: Not to exceed _____(5)_____ hours
Reasons for Overtime Required:
_____
_____
_____
_____
_____
_____

注：最后部分请写成段落。

高等学校英语应用能力考试（B级）
2015年12月真题

Part I Listening Comprehension (25 minutes)

Directions: This part is to test your listening ability. It consists of 4 sections.

Section A

Directions: This section is to test your ability to give proper responses. There are 7 recorded questions in it. After each question, there is a pause. The questions will be spoken two times. When you hear a question, you should decide on the correct answer from the 4 choices marked A), B), C) and D) given in your test paper. Then you should mark the corresponding letter on the Answer Sheet with a single line through the center.

1. A) Wonderful.
   B) Here you are.
   C) Thank you.
   D) I'll take one.

2. A) You can't miss it.
   B) It takes too much time.
   C) Nice to see you.
   D) Yes. it's John Smith.

3. A) How are you?
   B) Yes, I do.
   C) Here it is.
   D) My pleasure.

4. A) I'd love to.
   B) Take it easy.
   C) Five more minutes, please.
   D) The department managers.

5. A) That's too late.
   B) On Monday morning.
   C) Not bad.
   D) 45 Dollars.

6. A) Sure.
   B) Enjoy your dinner.
   C) Have a good time.
   D) Two single rooms, please.

7. A) On the third floor.
   B) Mind your steps.
   C) No problem.
   D) This way, please.

Section B

Directions: This section is to test your ability to understand short dialogues. There are 7 recorded dialogues in it. After each dialogue, there is a recorded question. Both the dialogues and questions will be spoken two times. When you hear a question, you should decide on the correct answer from the 4 choices marked A), B), C) and D) given in your test paper. Then you should mark the corresponding letter on the Answer Sheet with a single line through the center. Now listen to the dialogues.

8. A) She moved to another city.
   B) The working condition was poor.
   C) She was tired of the job.
   D) The job was too challenging.
9. A) A pair of shoes.   C) A T-shirt.
   B) A pair of socks.   D) Blue jeans.
10. A) He's been late.   C) He's failed an interview.
    B) He's got a cold.   D) He's lost his job.
11. A) The flight time.   C) The after-sales service.
    B) The new model.   D) The meeting schedule.
12. A) It is a good working habit.   C) It is a waste of time.
    B) It is helpful for learning.   D) It is harmful to health.
13. A) The job is interesting. C) The salary is good.
    B) The boss is nice.   D) The office is nice.
14. A) Making a work plan.   C) Having a training course.
    B) Working on a new project. D) Asking for a pay rise.

Section C

Directions: *In this section, there are 2 recorded conversations. After each conversation, there are some recorded questions. Both the conversations and questions will be spoken two times. When you hear a question, you should decide on the correct answer from the 4 choices marked A), B), C) and D) given in your test paper. Then you should mark the corresponding letter on the Answer Sheet with a single line through the center. Now listen to the conversations.*

Conversation 1

15. A) One night.   C) Three nights.
    B) Two nights.   D) Four nights.
16. A) Behind the building.   C) In front of the building.
    B) Across the street.   D) Near the shopping mall.

Conversation 2

17. A) A day off.   C) A new position.
    B) A pay rise.   D) A paid holiday.

18. A) Two years.   C) Five years.
    B) Three years.   D) Eight years.
19. A) To send an email to general manager.
    B) To give the woman more responsibilities.
    C) To offer the woman a training opportunity.
    D) To discuss the matter with the HR manager.

Section D

Directions: *In this section you will hear a recorded short passage. The passage is printed in the test paper, but with some words or phrases missing. The passage will be read three times. During the second reading, you are required to put the missing words or phrases on the Answer Sheet in order of the numbered blanks according to what you hear. The third reading is for you to check you writing. Now the passage will begin.*

    Have you ever thought what keeps people happy in their work? We've recently __20__ a survey. Of course, salary is important. Apart from salary, what else makes people happy with their jobs? Now please look at the chart. You can see the __21__ factor is the opportunities to learn and grow. It represents __22__ percent of the people we asked. And 20 percent of the people say __23__ to achieve their goal is important. Our survey also shows that another two important factors are a good working relationship with co-workers and a good __24__.

Part II   Vocabulary & Structure (10 minutes)

Section A

Directions: *In this section, there are 10 incomplete sentences. You are required to complete each one by deciding on the most appropriate word or words from the 4 choices marked A), B), C) and D). Then you should mark the corresponding letter on the Answer Sheet with a single line through the center.*

25. Some of the employees in the company are _____ to work at flexible hours.
    A) taken   B) achieved   C) allowed   D) formed

26. Please call us for more information as our website is currently _____ construction.
    A) under   B) by   C) of   D) with

27. _____, the sales manager began his report with the statistics of last month's sales.
    A) By now   B) As usual   C) So far   D) At most

28. We really appreciate our working environment, in _____ there was open, friendly workplace communication.

  A) how   B) what   C) whom   D) which

29. A company meeting provides an opportunity to _____ ideas and discuss any problems that come up within the workplace.

  A) right   B) share   C) take   D) while

30. Big changes have taken place at the Marketing Department _____ the new manager came.

  A) before   B) after   C) since   D) while

31. He said he would continue to support us _____ we didn't break the rules.

  A) as well as   B) as soon as   C) as far as   D) as long as

32. The school was _____ in 1929 by a Chinese scholar.

  A) established   B) placed   C) imagined   D) made

33. We have reached an agreement _____ we should invest in the Internet-related business.

  A) what   B) where   C) that   D) as

34. _____ the excellent service, guests can enjoy delicious food in our restaurant.

  A) In place of   B) In addition to   C) In charge of   D) In case of

Section B

Directions: *There are 5 incomplete statements here. You should fill in each blank with the proper form of the word given in brackets. Write the word or words in the corresponding space on the Answer Sheet.*

35. We are looking forward to (receive) _____ your early reply.

36. The main purpose of (educate) _____ is to teach students to think for themselves.

37. I was told that their project (complete) _____ as week as scheduled.

38. It is (general) _____ believed that about 14% of new cars can have electrical problems.

39. As a newcomer, almost everything in the company seems to be (interest) _____ to me.

Part Ⅲ   Reading Comprehension (35 minutes)

Directions: *The part is to test your reading ability. There are 5 tasks for you to fulfill. You should read the reading materials carefully and do the tasks as you are instructed.*

Task 1

Directions: *After reading the following passage, you will find 5 questions or unfinished statements, numbered 40 to 44. For each question or statement, there are 4 choices marked A), B), C) and D). You should make the correct choice and mark the corresponding letter on the Answer Sheet with a single line through the center.*

Starting a restaurant can be rewarding but challenging. Here are some steps to help you to make your restaurant business a success.

First, take a look at the restaurants that will be your competition. Learn what your competitors are serving and use the information to create a restaurant that will stand out among them. Speak to people to understand what type of restaurant they would like to have in the area.

Next, you will need to make a decision as to what kind of food you plan to offer. Choosing your target customers will help determine what type of food you will offer.

Research the different types of menus and select the menu items that will be right for your restaurant.

Deciding on the building and its location is also important for your success. Make sure that the building is easily found and reached. It is important to be located in an area that will attract customers.

Finally, do plenty of public relations work and advertisement of the restaurant opening. Consider having some special discounts and door prizes on the day of the grand opening.

40. According to the passage, the first step in starting a restaurant is to _____.
    A) find a suitable location
    B) set up your profit goal
    C) learn much about your competitors
    D) advertise the opening of your restaurant

41. By choosing your target customer, you can _____.
    A) learn how much you can charge for each dish
    B) decide on what kind of food to offer them
    C) know the cost of running the restaurant
    D) predict how many customers will arrive

42. Which of the following is important when you choose a building for your restaurant?
    A) There are no other restaurant nearby.
    B) It is easy for customers to visit.
    C) There is a parking lot available.

D) It is popular with tourists.

43. On the day of the opening of your restaurant, you are advised to _____.

   A) show customers around the building

   B) invite some important persons

   C) offer some special discounts

   D) make an opening speech

44. The passage is mainly about _____.

   A) how to choose a restaurant location

   B) how to cut restaurant running costs

   C) how to attract customers

   D) how to start a restaurant

Task 2

Directions: *The following is a poster. After reading it, you will find 3 questions or unfinished statements, numbered 45 to 47. For each question or statement there are 4 choices marked A), B), C) and D). You should make the correct choice and mark the corresponding letter on the Answer Sheet with a single line through the center.*

45. Which of the following is advertised in the poster?

   A) An arts exhibition.   C) A sport event. p.m.

   B) A furniture shop.   D) A garage sale.

46. According to the poster, the money to be raised will be given to _____.
   A) a high school   C) a local hospital
   B) a teen center   D) a local newspaper

47. If you register before April 17, the registration fee is _____.
   A) $20   B) $25   C) $30   D) $35

Task 3

Directions: *Read the following passage. After reading it, you should complete the information by filling in the blanks marked 48 to 52* (**in no more than 3 words**) *in the table below. You should write your answers on the Answer Sheet correspondingly.*

Using Best Buy Express Service is easy. Just follow the Purchasing Guide. Or contact us if you need more help. Please call 1-866-Best Buy with your questions.

The prices of Best Buy Express products are updated daily from BestBuy.com.

All Best Buy Express transactions are safe and secure. Any personal information you give us will be handled in the strictest confidence according to our Privacy Policy available at www.bestbuy.com. $2,000 limit per transaction.

If something is not right with your purchase, simply return your item(s) to one of our Best Buy stores in the Unites States. Returns will only be processed starting from the day following your purchase. Best Buy will be pleased to exchange or give you a refund in any Best Buy store in the United States. The sales receipt will be required to process a return.

Best Buy Express Service

How to use: follow the __48__

How to contact: call __49__

Prices of products: updated __50__ from BestBuy.com

Security & Privacy:
1) personal information: handled in the strictest confidence
2) Per transaction limit:$2,000

Returns:
1) where to return: any Best Buy store in the United States
2) when to process returns: from the day following __51__
3) what to be required to process a return: __52__

Task 4

Directions: *The following is a list of expressions often used for road signs. After* reading it, you are required to find the items equivalent to those given in Chinese in the table below. Then you should mark the corresponding letters in order of the numbered blanks, 53 through 57, on the Answer Sheet.

A—Don't follow too closely　　J—Electronic toll collection (ETC)
B—Keep distance　　K—Service area
C—Accident area　　L—No passing
D—Road closed　　M—No parking
E—Road work ahead　　N—Dead end
F—Two-way traffic　　O—No horn
G—One-way traffic　　P—Falling rocks
H—Bend ahead　　Q—Slow down at exit
I—Bus lane

Examples:(Q) 出口慢行	(M)（禁止泊车）
53. (　　) 单向行驶	(　　) 事故多发地
54. (　　) 电子收费	(　　) 小心岩石滑落
55. (　　) 前方弯道	(　　) 服务区
56. (　　) 保持车距	(　　) 公共车专用车道
57. (　　) 禁止鸣号	(　　) 前方道路封闭

Task 5

Directions: *Read the following passage. After reading it, you are required to complete the answers that follow the questions (No. 58 to No.62). You should write your answers* **(in no more than 3 words)** *on the Answer Sheet correspondingly.*

Public Storage is an international self-storage company. It rents spaces, ranging from closet-sized (橱柜大小的) units to ones that can hold the contents of a five-bedroom house. We offer indoor and outdoor business units—some with climate control—that have drive-up, walk-up and elevator access and convenient access hours.

Once you find the right storage space, reserve the self-storage unit online for free. Feel free to inspect the space and meet the property manager before renting the storage unit. When you're ready to pack, we've got everything you need, including the moving supplies.

Once you move in, you keep the only key to your self-storage unit, which you can access on your schedule. All of our business storage agreements are month-to-month, and you can change your storage unit space and location without penalty. Easy and flexible—that's what you can expect from Public Storage.

58. What kind of business units does Public Storage offer?

Public Storage offers _____ business units.

59. How can customers reserve the self-storage unit?

They can reserve it _____ for free.

60. What are you advised to do before renting the storage unit?

To inspect the space and meet _____.

61. What will Public Storage promise to do if you get ready to pack?

They will provide everything, include _____.

62. When can customers keep the key to their self-storage unit?

As soon as they _____.

Part Ⅳ Translation—English into Chinese (25 minutes)

Directions: This part, numbered 63 to 67, is to test your ability to translate English into Chinese. Each of the four sentences (No.63 to No.66) is followed by three choices of suggested translation marked A), B) and C). Make the best choice and write the corresponding letter on the Answer Sheet with a single line through the center. And then write your translation of the paragraph (No.67) in the corresponding space on the Translation/Composition Sheet.

63. Before developing their new project, the management team had thoroughly examined the organization's current situation.

A) 在开发新的项目之前，管理团队全面审视了该机构的现状。

B) 管理团队要先研究策略，才能清楚地了解公司产品的情况。

C) 要研发新的产品，管理团队需仔细地摸清公司原先的状况。

64. Our goal is to help business owners and professionals to master the art of effective communication.

A) 我们公司近期的目标是希望能找到具有沟通能力的专业人员。

B) 我们的宗旨是帮助企业主以及专业人士掌握有效交流的艺术。

C) 我们的目的是帮助公司老板与专家熟悉情况，提高沟通效率。

65. With over 60,000 products available, we are able to provide you with the top brand names on the market.

A) 我们能为你们提供市场上各种品牌，已拥有超过六万多的商品。

B) 我们将继续为你们提供各种产品，争取总量能达到六万多种。

C) 我们拥有六万多个产品，可以向你们提供市场上的顶级品牌。

66. The training course is designed for managers who want to increase their confidence and understand different marketing styles.

A) 本培训课程是为那些需要提高自信和了解不同营销风格的经理们而

设计的。

B) 本培训课程的目的是提高员工自信心，使他们了解不同的市场销售手段。

C) 本培训课程由经理设计，使员工掌握各种营销手段，用以提高他们的能力。

67. We repair computers of all brands. We provide you with professional advice, saving you both time and money in the long run. Our team understands technology well enough to make most computer systems work better.

Bring your computer in for a Free Check-Up, and we will recommend the most efficient way to solve your problems. We will only charge money if we can provide you with results!

Part V   Writing (25 minutes)

Directions: *This part is to test your ability to do practical writing. You are required to complete a form according to the following information given in Chinese. Remember to do your writing on the Translation /Composition Sheet.*

说明：假定你是李俊，请根据下列内容填写请假申请表。

姓名：李俊

员工号：120485

所在部门：市场部（Marketing Department）

请假类别：病假（Sick Leave）

拟请假日期：2016 年 1 月 10—24 日

请假理由：

在过去数周本人身体一直不适。由于本人在外地出差，无法及时就医。出差回来后，根据医生建议，需住院检查并治疗。请假时间为 2 周。

Leave Request Form	
Employee Information **Name:** ___(1)___ **Employee Number:** ___(2)___ **Department:** ___(3)___	
Leave Type: ___(4)___	
Starting Date: ___(5)___	**Resumption Date:** January 25th, 2016
Reason for Leave:	

Signature of Applicant: Li Jun

Answer Key

Unit One

Part I Vocabulary & Structure

Section A

1-5   DBACB

6-10 DCABC

Section B

11. suggestion(s)   12. longer   13. helpful   14. to smoke   15. was asked

Part II Reading Comprehension

Task 1: 1-5: BADAD

Task 2: 6-10: CBACB

Task 3

11. Communication Training Program   12. online   13. friendly

14. customer-friendly   15. the website

Task 4

16. H, F   17. K, D   18. J, E   19. A, G   20. M, N

Task 5

21. computer engineer   22. operating IBM PCs   23. 4

24. fluent   25. (they are) requested

Part III Translation (English into Chinese)

1. CBA   2. CBA   3. BCA   4. CBA

5. 兹证明病人托马斯先生，男，41岁，因患急性阑尾炎，于2000年6月9日住院。经立即施行手术和十天治疗后，现已痊愈，将于2000年6月19日出院。建议在家休息一个星期后再上班工作。

Part IV Practical Writing

Lost and Found

A lady has picked a wrist watch in the shopping center and turned it over to our office. The owner of the wrist watch may come to claim it with his or her identification card.

Lost and Found Office

Unit Two

Part I Vocabulary & Structure

Section A

1-5   ACDBD

6-10   ACBAD

Section B

11. Surprisingly   12. to assist   13. more effective   14. impression   15. meeting

Part II Reading Comprehension

Task 1: 1-5: CADCD

Task 2: 6-10: CDADB

Task 3

11. their preference   12. university and local   13. unfurnished

14. all-boys building   15. trash and water

Task 4

16. B, I   17. J, N   18. M, L   19. Q, O   20. A, H

Task 5

21. Miss Maria Wongs   22. Public Relations Officer

23. donated 100 books   24. twenty thousand

25. social gatherings

Part III Translation (English into Chinese)

1. BAC   2. CAB   3. ACB   4. BCA

5. 感谢您在访问伦敦期间选择我们的餐馆用餐。服务顾客是我们的主要工作。能够有机会为您服务我们倍感荣幸。我们真诚地欢迎您对我们的服务提出宝贵意见，并希望能了解您的用餐体验。请您花几分钟的时间填写顾客反馈表，以便我们日后能更好地为您服务。

Part IV Practical Writing

December 21, 2008

Dear Ms. Costa,

　　I'm safely back to New York from the business trip to Paris. A thousand thanks to you for the hospitality during my stay there. The deep impression both you and your city left on me will definitely live with me forever.

　　I learned more than I expected from the trip to your factory and school and I really enjoyed visiting the castles.

Thank you again for your hospitality and wish to see you again someday.

Yours sincerely,
Thomas Black
Assistant manager of JKM

Unit Three

Part I   Vocabulary & Structure
Section A
1-5   DACCB
6-10   DBABC
Section B
11. careful   12. is designed   13. efficiently   14. discussion   15. will grow

Part II   Reading Comprehension
Task 1: 1-5: DBBDD
Task 2: 6-10: CCABA
Task 3
11. permanent   12. the NBMC Series   13. wise and nutritional
14. affects   15. food preparation techniques
Task 4
16. F, P   17. G, H   18. E, K   19. N, L   20. B, O
Task 5
21. taste and manners   22. asking for advice   23. go
24. politely but firmly   25. perfectly acceptable

Part III   Translation (English into Chinese)
1. CBA   2. CAB   3. BCA   4. ACB
5. 《学生报》欲招聘一名记者。申请人需为在校大学生，有至少一年撰写新闻报道的经历。受聘人员的工作是报道发生在本市和校园的事件。如果您有意向，就请您于六月底之前将申请寄往《学生报》办公室。如需要更多相关信息，敬请访问我们的网站。

Part IV   Practical Writing

Dec. 19th, 2010

Dear Sirs and Madams concerned,

    I am writing to apply for the position of a secretary, which you advertised in China Daily on Dec. 10th, 2010.

    I graduated from Dongfang University last year. While in college I majored in Business Administration and I got the certificate of English band 4 and 6, and that of computer. As you can see from my resume, I once worked as a part time staff in DDF Company. I am skilled at the operation of computer, and I have some work experience in dealing with office affairs.

I would be available for an interview at your request. Please contact me at 86547782 and thank you for your consideration of my application.

Enclosed please find my resume.

Best wishes.

Sincerely yours,

Wang Lin

Unit Four

Part I Vocabulary & Structure

Section A

1-5   CABDB

6-10   CDACB

Section B

11. receiving   12. education   13. was completed   14. generally   15. interesting

Part II Reading Comprehension

Task 1: 1-5: BADCC

Task 2: 6-10: DBCBA

Task 3

11. characters   12. caring   13. society   14. contact

15. community

Task 4

16. O, A   17. J, M   18. B, I   19. G, F   20. P, E

Task 5

21. artificial Christmas trees   22. competitive

23. its customers   24. Europe   25. 2.2%

Part III Translation (English into Chinese)

1. CBA   2. BAC   3. BCA   4. CBA

5. 感谢您昨日参加在我们办公室举行的求职面试。我们将在两周之内通知您我们对您的申请做出的决定。我们想让您知道我们会认真考虑您的求职申请。如果由于某种原因我们此次无法向您提供职位，我们会记录下您的这次面试申请。一旦有职位空缺，我们就会立刻通知您。

Part IV Practical Writing

Invitation Letter

December 20, 2009

Mr. Mike Kennedy
General Manager
UST Electronics Corporation
Dear Mr. Zhang,

  The purpose of this letter is to formally invite you to attend our 30th anniversary dinner party which is planned to be held at Holiday Inn at 7 p.m. on Tuesday, Dec. 29th, 2009.

  We'd like to take this opportunity to express our sincere thanks to you for your support and cooperation in these past years.

  In closing, we would be very pleased and honored if you would consent to be with us at the party.

Yours sincerely,
Mike Kennedy
General Manager
UST Electronics Corporation

Unit Five

Part I Vocabulary & Structure
Section A
1-5   BACBA
6-10   CDCBA
Section B
11. to guess   12. be made   13. frequently   14. agreement   15. more difficult

Part II Reading Comprehension
Task 1: 1-5: DBCCD
Task 2: 6-10: DABBB
Task 3
11. 120   12. 50.60   13. First National City Bank
14. Item A and B   15. the shipping mark
Task 4
16. I, M   17. B, J   18. K, C   19. D, H   20. E, L
Task 5
21. Valentine's   22. red wine   23. 10-minute

24. Bank of China   25. send it back

Part Ⅲ   Translation (English into Chinese)

1. CAB   2. CAB   3. ABC   4. CAB

5. "就业与培训"是一个求职和学习的网站，它为网上求职者提供最受欢迎的服务，使你轻而易举地获得你所需要的信息。在这个网站，你会发现 30 多万份工作、成千上万的培训机会以及人才市场的信息。由于"就业与培训"网利用了互联网的强大效力，它比以往任何时候能更迅速、更容易地为你提供你所需要的一切信息。

Part Ⅳ   Practical Writing

Notice

  Dong Fang Electronics Ltd. is a joint venture, which mainly produces electronic products. Its recruitment meeting will be held at our students' club on December 26 of 2007 (Wednesday). The vacant positions include office secretary, marketing employees and laboratory technicians. Students who are interested in it are expected to attend the recruitment meeting in Room 2, at 1:30 in the afternoon. ID card, resume, and the certificates of PET (level B) & computer are required.

Students' Union
December 16, 2007

Unit Six

Part Ⅰ   Vocabulary & Structure

Section A

1-5   BCADC

6-10   ABDDA

Section B

11. seriously   12. be raised   13. personal   14. more effective   15. differences

Part Ⅱ   Reading Comprehension

Task 1: 1-5   CBCCC

Task 2: 6-10   BBCDC

Task 3

11. drinking   12. 16 and 18   13. at night   14. left side

15. pocket

Task 4

16. D, I   17. B, E   18. L, M   19. O, G   20. P, J

Task 5

21. their participation   22. the exhibition

23. four days 24. the marketing campaign
25. display area

Part Ⅲ Translation (English into Chinese)
1. CBA   2. BAC   3. CBA   4. BCA
5. 如果你想得到驾驶执照，你得去驾驶执照办公室申请，为了在该地区驾驶汽车，你会被要求参加一个笔试/你会被要求参加笔试，以便能在该地区开车。你还需要通过一次视力检测。如果需要戴眼镜，你就必须得戴眼镜，此外，你还必须通过实际驾车考试。如果你的笔试和实驾考试不及格，你可以另找一天再参加考试。

Part Ⅳ Practical Writing

March 15, 2011

Dear Tracy,

　　How have you been? Haven't seen you for nearly two years after graduation. I heard that you would come to Nanjing for a business trip. How about coming to see me and letting me accompany you to visit Xuanwu Lake and Dr. Sun Yat-sen's Mausoleum?

　　Hope to hear from you soon!

Yours,
Sharon

Unit Seven

Part Ⅰ Vocabulary & Structure
Section A
1-5   DBACB
6-10 DCACB
Section B
11. to check   12. finally   13. was established   14. leaving   15. useful

Part Ⅱ Reading Comprehension
Task 1: 1-5   ADDAB
Task 2: 6-10   BCCAB
Task 3
11. bottle of medicine   12. 3
13. reduce the amount   14. drink
15. not above 25℃
Task 4
16. G, E   17. N, K   18. C, O   19. A, D   20. L, M
Task 5
21. teaching English   22. relevant certificates

23. at all levels   24. teaching children

25. the challenge

Part Ⅲ Translation (English into Chinese)

1. BCA   2. ACB   3. CBA   4. CAB

5. 如今，人们可以选择工作地点和工作种类，因此，人们面临的挑战是决定去哪里工作。人们需要了解做决定时所需要的标准。本书为人们做决定提供了非常实用的建议。同时，人们也能了解要问哪些问题，要寻找什么样的工作以及如何做出最后的决定。

Part Ⅳ Practical Writing

Dear Mr. Baker,

  Welcome to Fuzhou!

  We have reserved for you a room in Oriental Hotel which is 20 kilometers away from the International Airport. You can reach there by taxi or shuttle bus.

  I hope to see you at my office at 10 a.m. the following morning after you get here.

  Please do not hesitate to contact me at 5757517 if you need any help.

Yours sincerely,
Wang Dong
Staff of Hongxia Trading Company

Unit Eight

Part Ⅰ Vocabulary & Structure

Section A

1-5   ADABC

6-10   ABCAD

Section B

11. quickly   12. washed   13. to build   14. interesting   15. better

Part Ⅱ Reading Comprehension

Task 1: 1-5   CAABB

Task 2: 6-10   BCCBA

Task 3

11. 48 hours   12. lukewarm water   13. suitable gloves

14. eyelashes and eyebrows   15. children

Task 4

16. C, I   17. O, G   18. F, L   19. D, H   20. P, A

Task 5

21. International Trade   22. leading exporters

23. Pure silk   24. the traditional skills

25. A catalog

Part III Translation (English into Chinese)

1. CAB 2. ABC 3. BCA 4. ABC

5. 为我们的员工提供最好的技术支持服务是我们的责任。我们正在努力明确所提供的每一项服务的信息。同时我们以实现最高的服务标准为目标。然而，请记住事情有时可能会出错。如果这种情况发生了，请立刻拨打 01782294443 告知我们。我们将竭尽全力把事情处理好。

Part IV Practical Writing

The Internet is becoming more and more important in our daily life. On the net, we can learn news both at home and abroad and all kinds of other information as well. We can also send messages by e-mail, make phone calls, go to net school, read different kinds of books and learn foreign languages by ourselves. Besides, we can enjoy music, watch sports matches and play chess or cards. On the net, we can even do shopping, have a chat with others and make friends with them. In a word, the Internet has made our life more colorful.

Unit Nine

Part I Vocabulary & Structure

Section A

1-5   CDBAA

6-10   BCDCB

Section B

11. specially   12. trying   13. be held   14. to lock   15. possibility

Part II Reading Comprehension

Task 1: 1-5   BADCB

Task 2: 6-10   DCBAC

Task 3

11. companies   12. record

13. ensure   14. From

15. Subject

Task 4

16. G, H   17. B, L   18. M, I   19. K, P   20. Q, E

Task 5

21. the travel distance   22. at the destination

23. a travel card   24. tube stations

25. passport-size photograph

Part Ⅲ Translation (English into Chinese)

1. CBA   2. ABC   3. CAB   4. ABC

5. 快来参加我们的行走小组。在 11 周的活动中，我们将帮你改善健康。每周我们会有一个讲座或行走，教你更健康地生活。我们将举办一次配导游的购物旅游和多次有趣的指引徒步活动。此外，每个成员都会收到一些关于步行的纸质材料。

Part Ⅳ Practical Writing

April 10th, 2011

Dear Kate,

　　I'm sorry to tell you that I couldn't go to see the film with you this Sunday. My grandmother suddenly fell ill and was taken to hospital this morning. I have to take care of her this weekend. The doctor told us it will take about one week for her to get better. So I think we can go to the cinema together next weekend.

　　Please allow me to say sorry again!

Yours,
Li Feng

Unit Ten

Part Ⅰ Vocabulary & Structure

Section A

1-5　CAABD

6-10　ABDBC

Section B

11. treating　12. deeply　13. harder　14. equipment　15. has been working

Part Ⅱ Reading Comprehension

Task 1: 1-5　BCCAD

Task 2: 6-10　BCACD

Task 3

11. AAR Trade Company　　12. April 11, 2016

13. entered into　　14. The JV Company

15. this Agreement

Task 4

16. A, I　17. C, H　18. E, M　19. F, D　20. N, O

Task 5

21. an interview　　22. easy to read

23. phone number　　24. related experience

25. Yours sincerely

Part Ⅲ Translation (English into Chinese)
1. ACB   2. CBA   3. CAB   4. BAC

5. 现在人们可以选择去哪里工作和做何种工作。他们面临着决定去向的挑战。他们需要了解采用什么标准来做决定。本书给他们提供了做出选择的实用性建议。同时，他们还将会知道需要问什么问题，该找什么工作，以及如何做出最后的决定。

Part Ⅳ Practical Writing

April 8, 2014

Dear Miss Zhang,

    I am truly sorry that I can't go to school today. Yesterday on my way home, I fell off the bicycle and hurt my leg. Luckily, I wasn't badly hurt, and the doctor advised me to stay in bed and have a good rest. So I ask for three-day leave from April 8 to 10. I'll catch up with others when I am back to school.

Truly yours,

Wang Lin

2016年12月B级真题答案

Part Ⅰ Listening Comprehension

Section A   1-7   ACDBCAD

Section B   8-14   ACBDCAB

Section C   15-19   ADABD

Section D   20. express   21. be proud of   22. depend on

             23. ideas   24. once again

Part Ⅱ Vocabulary & Structure

Section A   25-29   ACDBD

            30-34   ACBAD

Section B   35. Surprisingly   36. to assist   37. more effective

            38. impression   39. meeting

Part Ⅲ Reading Comprehension

Task 1   40-44 DCBBA

Task 2   45-47 BCC

Task 3

48. Committee Members   49. March 7-11   50. Omni Houston

51. US $139   52. IEEE Transformers

Task 4

53. M, D   54. Q, H   55. A, K   56. C, I   57. E, F

Task 5

58. any network   59. operating system   60. on the receipt

61. very rude   62. copy

Part Ⅳ Translation—English into Chinese

63. BCA   64. ACB   65. CAB   66. CBA

67. 道路建设将于 2017 年 1 月 9 日星期一开始。预计持续一个月。第七街与第九街之间的区域将完全封闭。

我们为可能造成的不便表示歉意，但施工的目的是使道路更安全。谢谢您的理解。

如果您对该次施工有疑问的话，请拨打电话（650）903-6311。

Part Ⅴ Writing

Overtime Request Form

Request Date: (1) March 1, 2017

Employee's Name: (2) Li Jianxin

Department: (3) Human Resources Department

Date of Overtime: March 5, 2017

Overtime Needed: From (4) 9:00 a.m. to 5:00 p.m.

Total Overtime: Not to exceed (5) 8 Hours

Reasons for Overtime Required:

Our company is recruiting employees to fill vacations recently. Human Resources Department inserted an advertisement in the newspaper a week ago, and has received application letters. In order to assist all departments to arrange interviews and visits to various sites, I need to work overtime on Saturday to learn more about candidates and then arrange interviews.

2015 年 12 月 B 级真题答案

Part Ⅰ Listening Comprehension

Section A 1-7   ADBACAA

Section B 8-14   BABCDCB

Section C 15-19 BABCD

Section D 20. carried   21. bigger   22. 28

           23. the ability   24. working condition

Part Ⅱ Vocabulary & Structure

Section A 25-29 CABDB

30-34　CDACB

Section B　35. receiving　　　36. education　　　37. had been completed

　　　　　38. generally　　　　39. interesting

Part Ⅲ　Reading Comprehension

Task 1　40-44 CBBCD

Task 2　45-47 DBA

Task 3

48. Purchasing Guide　　　49. 1-866-Best Buy　　　50. daily

51. your purchase　　　　52. the sales receipt

Task 4

53. G, C　　　54. J, P　　　55. H, K　　　56. B, I　　　57. O, D

Task 5

58. indoor and outdoor　　59. online　　　60. the property manager

61. the moving supplies　　62. move in

Part Ⅳ　Translation—English into Chinese

63. ACB　　　64. BCA　　　65. CAB　　　66. ABC

67. 我们维修各种品牌电脑。提供专业建设，从长远看，为您节省时间和金钱。我们的团队技术精湛，足以让大多数的电脑系统更好运行。

　　免费检测电脑，并向您推荐最有效的办法，解决您的问题。我们只在修复电脑之后收取费用。

Part Ⅴ　Writing

Leave Request Form
Employee Information
Name: (1) Li Jun
Employee Number: (2) 120485
Department: (3) Marketing Department
Leave Type: (4) Sick Leave
Starting Date: (5) January 10th, 2016　　**Resumption Date**: January 25th, 2016
Reason for Leave: 　　I've not been quite well in the past few weeks. As I was out on business travel, I didn't see the doctor in time. After coming back, I went to hospital. According to the doctor's suggestion, I should stay in hospital to have a further examination. I would like to ask for sick leave of 2 weeks, i.e. from January 10th to January 24th. I should be very much obliged if you will grant me my request. **Signature of Applicant**: Li Jun

参考文献

[1] 谈芳,等. 全国高等学校英语应用能力考试全真模拟试题及详解 B 级[M]. 上海：学林出版社，2014.

[2] 李庆杰. 备战高等学校英语应用能力考试 B 级过关必备历年真题与详解[M]. 北京：世界知识出版社，2016.

[3] 李成华. 星火英语 AB 级试卷真题详解+标准预测（B 级）[M]. 上海：上海交通大学出版社，2018.

[4] 陈战. 星火英语 AB 级试卷高等学校应用能力考试 B 级真题点评 [M]. 长春：吉林出版集团有限责任公司，2011.

[5] 李丽春，李买燕，李睿. 高等学校英语应用能力考试（A&B 级）真题+模拟[M]. 北京：北京理工大学出版社，2017.

[6] 高等学校英语应用能力考试命题研究中心. 高等学校英语应用能力考试 B 级解题技巧及试题解析[M]. 北京：北京理工大学出版社，2016.

[7] 崔艳萍，冯新艳. 高等学校英语应用能力考试（B 级）真题精讲[M]. 第 2 版. 北京：外语教学与研究出版社，2014.

[8] 高等学校英语应用能力考试研究中心. 高等学校英语应用能力考试 B 级历年真题详解[M]. 北京：外文出版社，2017.

[9] 江利娟，张明宏. 高等学校英语应用能力 B 级考试全真模拟训练及详解[M]. 苏州：苏州大学出版社，2016.

[10] 王勇，胡焱. 高等学校英语应用能力等级考试 B 级历年真题精编[M]. 上海：上海交通大学出版社，2017.

[11] 赵丽萍. 高等学校英语 B 级考试真题、模拟及解析[M]. 天津：天津大学出版社，2015.

[12] 杨静怡. 全国高等学校英语应用能力考试 B 级历年真题及解析[M]. 上海：同济大学出版社，2012.

[13] 张大为，张步寅，吕进. 高等学校英语应用能力考试 B 级辅导[M]. 长春：东北师范大学出版社，2015.

[14] 张玲，纪淑军. B 级考试历年真题解析与模拟试卷[M]. 北京：中国人民大学出版社，2012.

[15] 赵晓敏，张艳霜. 高等学校英语应用能力 B 级考试过关必做 1200 题[M]. 北京：中国石化出版社，2014.

[16] 李秀明，张捷，冯修文. 最新英语应用能力考试（B 级）考前冲刺模拟题集[M]. 北京：高等教育出版社，2016.

[17] http://www.jokeawhenever.com/inspirational/136-the-water-of-life-it.html
[18] http://www.livinglifefully.com/zineu26may.htm#Eyes%20Wide%20Open
[19] http://www.livinglifefully.com/zineu16jun.htm#Eyes%20Wide%20Open
[20] http://www.livinglifefully.com/zine.htm
[21] http://myselfdevelopment.net
[22] http://blog.360.yahoo.com/
[23] http://www.beliefnet.com
[24] http://www.tingclass.net/
[25] http://www.kekenet.com/
[26] http://www.putclub.com/
[27] http://bridge.toeic.cn/tutorial.aspx
[28] http://www.hjenglish.com/
[29] http://www.51ielts.com/
[30] https://www.langeasy.com.cn/